OTHER BOOKS FROM BITTERROOT MOUNTAIN PUBLISHING

Bitterroot Mountain Authors, Phantasma 1
2013, ISBN 978-1-940025-06-3, Kindle

Neil Bricco, Wisdom of the Wound, 2013, ISBN 978-1-940025-00-1, Kindle
Neil Bricco, Wisdom of the Wound
2013, ISBN 978-1-940025-01-8, Trade Paperback

Dr. Mark William Cochran, Oby's Wisdom
2012, ISBN 978-0-9852784-0-3, Kindle
Dr. Mark William Cochran, Oby's Wisdom
2010, ISBN 978-0-9817874-6-6, Trade Paperback

Patti Dickinson, Hollywood the Hard Way
2012, ISBN 978-0-9852784-2-7, Kindle
Patti Dickinson, Indian's Daughter
2011, ISBN 978-0-9817874-7-3, Trade Paperback
Patti Dickinson, Indian's Daughter
2011, ISBN 978-0-9817874-9-7, Kindle

Ana Parker Goodwin , Forbidden Justice
2012, ISBN 978-0-9852784-1-0, Kindle

Darla Isackson, Finding Hope While Grieving Suicide
2013, ISBN 978-1-940025-5, Kindle
Darla Isackson, Finding Hope While Grieving Suicide
2013, ISBN 978-1-940025-03-2, Trade Paperback

Larry Telles, A Brief History of the Silent Screen and the World at that Time,
2008, ISBN 978-0-9817874-0-4
Larry Telles, Helen Gibson, Silent Serial Queen
2012, ISBN 978-0-9852784-9-6, DVD
Larry Telles, Helen Gibson, Silent Serial Queen
2013, ISBN 978-0-9852784-6-5, Trade Paperback

Bobby Wilhelm, Bobby Convict
2012, ISBN 978-0-9852784-8-9, Trade Paperback
Bobby Wilhelm, Bobby Convict, 2012, ISBN 978-0-9852784-7-2, Hardcover
Bobby Wilhelm, Bobby Convict, 2012, ISBN 978-0-9852784-4-1, Nook
Bobby Wilhelm, Bobby Convict, 2012, ISBN 978-0-9852784-3-4, Kindle

AN OUNCE OF TRUTH

Bitterroot Mountain
Publishing

The Museum of North Idaho Collection

Cover Photograph - The Museum of North Idaho Collection

AN OUNCE OF TRUTH

Stories inspired by the Historic Jewett House

The Coeur d'Alene Idaho Writers League
Member 2017 Jewett House Anthology

Introduction
by
Historian Robert Singletary

Bitterroot Mountain
Publishing
Hayden, ID 83835

AN OUNCE OF TRUTH: Stories Inspired by the Historic Jewett House

Copyright © 2017 IWL Coeur d'Alene Chapter
Published by Bitterroot Mountain LLC - 9030 N. Hess Street,
Suite 331, Hayden, ID 83835

Front cover by Larry Telles and E.G. Moore
Interior Design by Larry Telles
Photographs: Robert Singletary and the CdA Museum.

This is a work of non-fiction and fiction. The introduction author and publisher have made every effort to ensure the accuracy and completeness of information contained in that section, we assume no responsibility for errors, inaccuracies, omissions, or any inconsistency herein. Any slights of people, places, or organizations are unintentional. The remaining portion of this book is pure fiction.

All rights reserved. No part of this book may be reproduced, stored in a retrieval system, or transmitted in any form or by any means—electronic, mechanical, digital, photocopy, recording, or any other—except for brief quotations in printed reviews, without prior written permission of the publisher. For information regarding permission for excerpts please contact Bitterroot Mountain Publishing at editor@BitterrootMountainLLC.com

First edition: 2017
ISBN 978-1-940025-31-5
Library of Congress Control Number 2017949305

Printed in the United States of America.

20 19 18 17 16 15 14 13 12 11 10 9 8 7 6 5 4 3 2 1

1. Jewett House History -- non-fiction. 2. Coeur d'Alene History -- non-fiction. 3. House by the Lake -- non-fiction. 4. Stories of the Jewett House -- fiction. 5. Stories of Coeur d'Alene, Idaho -- fiction. 6. Stories about the House by the Lake -- fiction. 7. Articles of the House by the Lake -- non-fiction. 8. Articles of Coeur d'Alene in 1915-1917 -- non-fiction.

This book is dedicated to those people
who love and cherish local
Coeur d'Alene history.

Table of Contents

Playing for Keeps   1
by Jennifer Lamont Leo

That House There by the Lake   9
By Emily Moore

Jewett House Josephine   10
by Josephie Jackson

The Parlor Window   15
by Terry Robinson

Elsie's Story   16
by Anna Goodwin

The 1916 – 1917 Summer Serenade   22
by Larry Telles

From the Legend of Blackjack Diamond   24
by Jesse Warburton

From the Legend of Blackjack Diamond   28
by Jesse Warburton

Beneath the Blue Damask   33
by Lila Bolme

Saying Goodbye to a First Love   34
by Becca Crouse

Celebration in Seventeen   38
By Tana Essary

Just Me, Marla 39
By Barbara K. Rostad

The Second Wednesday 48
by Terry Robinson

The Journey 49
by Larry Telles

If Timber Could Talk 57
by Jesse Warburton

Below Red Elevation 59
by E.G. Moore

Jewett House Nickel Tour 66
by Terry Robinson

The 1916 – 1917 Small Town Outlook 71
by Larry Telles

News Worth Living For 74
by E.G. Moore

Epilogue 78

Author Bios 79

TAKE TIME

Take time to laugh.
It is the music of the soul.
Take time to think.
It is the source of power.
Take time to play.
It is the source of perpetual youth.
Take time to read.
It is the fountain of wisdom.
Take time to pray.
It is the greatest power on Earth.
Take time to love and be loved.
It is a God-given privilege.
Take time to be friendly.
It is the road to happiness.
Take time to give.
It is too short a day to be selfish.
Take time to work.
It is the price of success.

- Anonymous

PREFACE

It isn't very often you hear of a 100 year anniversary. When you do, you take note. They won't come around again for a great while. I was made aware, late in 2016, that the beautiful, old Jewett House had made that milestone. I had been coming to that majestic house sitting by the lake since joining the Idaho Writers League in 2001. I had also been a guest speaker at our meetings where I stood and stared out the huge picture window at Lake Coeur d'Alene. Many times stopping my talk in mid-sentence, mesmerized by the beautiful scene before me.

As a writer, author, and illustrator, I could not let this 100 year event go quietly by without something to remember. Just after Christmas 2016, the idea popped into my head. I remembered that back in 2001 this chapter was challenged to write a book. At the time, the chapter members were reading their stories to the children of Children's Village in Coeur d'Alene. Those stories and poems were edited just as in the real world of book submissions. The finished book, Kaleidoscope: A Kollection of Tantalizing Tales became the finished product.

This time the Jewett House could be the recipient of the stories and tales inside a book. The profits from the book would be split evenly after publishing expenses. The Jewett House would use the funds to put on a 100 year birthday celebration in September. All of Coeur d'Alene would be invited.

In order to produce a book of this quality, there are people behind the scenes who help a great deal. We would like to thank the Jewett House Advisory Board: Marla Lake, John Boraas, Kay Nelson, Walt Melior, Nancy Wilson, Katie Sayler, and Warren Bakes. To add the historical element, Robert Singletary and Museum of North Idaho Director Dorothy Dahlgren. The four editors who double-checked the grammar and punctuation of the stories you are about to read: Amy Conley, Jenny Lamont Leo, Mary Langer Smith, and Emily Moore. Lastly, the Idaho Writers League Marketing person, Ron Vergona.

Robert Singletary gave us the house history. The Jewett House board and the Idaho Writers League Coeur d'Alene Chapter worked out the details. To complete the book process, Bitterroot Mountain Publishing donated the ISBN, bar code, and time for formatting the interior of the book. You have the results in your hands.

Larry Telles
July 1, 2017

FOREWORD

It's not every day that a house turns 100 years old. It's even less often that when a house does, it still stands proud and strong, a piece of living history. The Jewett House is a community icon, maintained by those who love it as equally as those who built it in 1917. This anthology in your hand presents a unique opportunity for the buyer: to invest in history, to be a part of it in more ways than one. Within the pages of this book, you'll find stories, poems, and non-fiction all dedicated to the historic inspiration of this beautiful house. Each holds an ounce of truth, a small piece of the house wrapped in words meant to entertain and inform you. Whether you love sweet love stories, dark fantastical tales, ruffians or widows, re-imagined futures of the Pacific Northwest, or the history of music from a piano's point of view, you'll find a favorite among the 20+ pieces written by members of the Idaho Writers League Coeur d'Alene chapter.

Fifty percent of the profits will go back into the celebration and care of the Jewett House. Won't you be a part of the local people dedicated to this local cause?

E.G. Moore
July 1. 2017

INTRODUCTION

THE JEWETT HOUSE

With major historical events such as the construction of Fort Sherman, the discovery of gold and silver, and the development of towns taking place in northern Idaho, government agents under the leadership of forester John B. Leiberg were surveying the Northwest for marketable timber. When Leiberg's report was made public in 1898, several eastern lumber companies started a major timber boom in the Coeur d'Alene region. One of those companies was the Edward Rutledge Lumber Company from Rutledge, Minnesota. Timber baron Frederick Weyerhaeuser had a major investment in the Rutledge Company. During the early 1900s, Rutledge with the backing of Weyerhaeuser, started purchasing acres and acres of timber land in the Coeur d'Alenes. However, the Rutledge sawmill did not start operating until 1916.

The Rutledge plant and lumber yards were located on the present site of the Coeur d'Alene Resort Golf Course. While the mill was under construction, the company also started building a home for the general manager of the Rutledge plant. The home was completed in 1917 and located at 1501 East Lakeshore Drive, just west of the mill site. Huntington Taylor and his family were the first occupants of the company house. Taylor was brought from Wisconsin to supervise the construction of the new plant and became the first general manager.

The design of the company house was known as American Foursquare, which was a popular design from the 1890s to the 1930s. Typical of this architectural style, the Rutledge Company house was simple in form, square in shape with a hipped roof and dormers on the top floor. The original porch was built of wood with a gabled roof above the entry. At the east end of the porch was an attached covered drive through.

Huntington Taylor was the general manager of Rutledge until 1928. He was succeeded by George "Fritz" Jewett, the grandson of Frederick Weyerhaeuser. Jewett and his family lived in the company house until 1937 when they bought a home in Spokane. After the Jewett family moved to Spokane the company house was no longer used as a private residence. Beginning in 1940 it became a staff house and was used to entertain company officials and international guests until 1972.

The Museum of North Idaho Collection

In 1978 the "Jewett House" was granted to the City of Coeur d'Alene with a deed of trust that provided the house would be used as a senior center. Today the Jewett House is still owned by the City of Coeur d'Alene. A Jewett House Board is appointed by the Mayor and City Council to advise the city on the use and maintenance of the Jewett House Senior Center.

Robert Singletary
July 18, 2017

AN OUNCE OF TRUTH BEGINS

Playing for Keeps

by Jennifer Lamont Leo

"Next stop, Rathdrum, Idaho."

At the conductor's bellow, I consulted the dog-eared Northern Pacific timetable clutched in my damp palm, then stared out the train's grimy window. After three days on the North Coast Limited, it hardly seemed possible I'd arrived at last. A shiver of delight coursed down my spine.

I peered into the little mirror glued inside the lid of my travel case. Hair combed, check. Face washed, check. My complexion looked pale, and faint shadows ringed my eyes, but there was nothing to be done about that. At fifteen I was too young to wear face powder. Or so decreed my stepmother, Frances.

An hour earlier I'd latched myself into the restroom and changed into a fresh dress—blue cotton with embroidered cuffs and a white rolled collar. I yearned to show my old friend, Maisie Summerfield, that I was no longer a dungaree-wearing tomboy, at least not all the time.

But a change of clothes did only so much good. Frankly, I needed a long, hot bath. Did the Summerfields even have a bathtub? Out in the untamed Idaho wilderness, a luxurious modern amenity like indoor plumbing might not be a given. I knew this thanks to my fondness for dime novels in which plucky spinsters headed West to escape overbearing relatives and found primitive living conditions-along with romance, if they were lucky, which they usually were.

In her letters, Maisie had gushed about thick forests, towering mountains, and sparkling lakes. While she never stated outright that her family lived in a rustic log cabin tucked away in the backcountry, I could read between the lines. I imagined her churning butter and chopping wood—an impression strengthened as the train chugged through the rugged Northern Rockies.

I stiffened my spine. If a hot bath was not to be had, I vowed to be gracious and uncomplaining. Hardships were to be expected as part of this great Idaho adventure. It would be fun, like last summer's trip to Camp Minne-WaWa, minus the poison ivy.

I snapped the case shut. I'd looked forward to this trip for weeks, ever since Frances had received a letter from Mrs. Summerfield inviting me to spend part of summer vacation with her daughter. Maisie had been my best chum at Kerryville Grammar School until three years ago, when her father's new job with a big lumber mill uprooted her family to Idaho. When our teacher pointed to Idaho on the schoolroom map, my heart sank at the vast distance between there and Illinois.

At last the engine steamed into the Rathdrum depot. I swiped at the smudged window with my hankie and thought of my last conversation with Maisie at the Kerryville station.

"You'll write to me?" Her eyes had looked suspiciously misty.

"Of course, silly. Every week."

I'd meant it, too. At first our letters had flown thick and fast. But then school and dramatics club and baseball practice had eaten up my time. Maisie was busy, too. Gradually our letters dwindled from weekly to once-in-a-while.

But that was all about to change. Now we'd pick up our friendship exactly where we'd left off. I reached into my pocket and fingered the gift I'd brought: a hefty, cobalt-blue cats-eye marble, a real beauty of a shooter. I'd coveted it for a long time, and finally won it fair and square from Sammy Wardlow while playing for keeps. Now I was giving it to Maisie, because if ever a girl was an ace at shooting marbles, it was her.

Anxiously I scanned the platform. Only a few people stood waiting: a man wearing a brown fedora pulled down over his eyes, another man in overalls, and two well-dressed ladies standing together. No sign of Maisie.

I peered again at the man in the fedora. Perhaps Maisie's father had been sent to fetch me. But this man didn't look like Mr. Summerfield, as best I could recall. I swallowed hard. What if everyone forgot I was coming?

My gaze slid back to the two ladies, and my heart lurched. It wasn't two ladies: it was Maisie and her mother. Maisie was practically grown-up!

I stood, grabbed my case, and followed the other passengers off the train.

"Hello!" I shouted, waving my arm.

Maisie whirled around. "Helen! There you are."

I dropped the case and flew at my friend, enveloping her in an ecstatic hug that knocked her hat askew. As we embraced, I noticed two things: how very tall Maisie had gotten, and how she was surrounded by the scent of roses. As for myself, I was certain I must stink to high heaven of soot and axle grease and worse.

"Let me look at you." Maisie held me at arm's length, eyes sparkling. "It's so lovely to see you."

"And how!" I returned the grin, but suddenly felt awkward. So lovely to see you? Since when did Maisie say things like so lovely to see you? That was grown-up talk. Who was this stranger?

We stood gawking at each other like goofs. Not only was my friend tall and rose-scented, but she wore lip rouge the color of ripe strawberries, and her formerly waist-length hair had been chopped short around her ears, topped by a fashionable cloche. My own lips were bare, and my locks hung in two childish braids down my back, bobbed hair and lip rouge being two more things that Frances didn't approve of.

Mrs. Summerfield kissed my cheek. "You must be exhausted after your trip, Helen, dear," she said in her gracious way.

Yes. Yes, that was it. I was tired. Everything would seem less strange after a good rest. And a bath, because it was clear from Maisie's appearance that the Summerfields did indeed own a bathtub.

After we'd collected my luggage, Mrs. Summerfield led the way toward a shiny silver roadster parked nearby.

I blinked. "Jeepers. This is yours?"

Maisie laughed and said, "Of course. What did you expect? A lumber truck?"

I echoed her laugh and adjusted my assumptions. I watched in admiration as Mrs. Summerfield slid behind the wheel. Not many women back in Kerryville drove their own automobiles.

We drove across a flat prairie ringed with mountains, then into the bustling town of Coeur d'Alene. My shyness faded as Maisie prattled on, asking questions about my trip and about people we both knew back home. I found it easier to talk to her if I kept my gaze on the scenery instead of on the poised and polished stranger sitting beside me.

Mrs. Summerfield pointed out the newly built Federal Building and Courthouse, as imposing and governmental-looking as anything back east. Sherman Avenue was lined on either side with intriguing-looking shops and cafes, even a movie theater. To my surprise, Coeur d'Alene didn't look much different from Kerryville, except for the mountains.

"Here we are," Mrs. Summerfield said at last, pulling into the driveway of a splendid white American foursquare with a wide, inviting porch and an emerald lawn that swept clear down to the sparkling waters of Lake Coeur d'Alene.

The last shred of my log-cabin vision whirled away on the lake breeze. Whatever Mr. Summerfield's job was over at that logging mill, he clearly didn't do it in sap-stained overalls.

Mrs. Summerfield gave me a quick tour of the spacious downstairs rooms, filled with sunlight and smelling of lemon oil and beeswax. Then she suggested I take a rest before dinner. Maisie helped me unpack in her sunny bedroom overlooking the lake.

"Spiffy," she commented, shaking out my yellow dress with appliquéd daisies and hanging it in the closet. "You can wear it to the party tonight."

I yawned. "What party?"

She picked up another garment. "Mother thought it would be a good idea to have some friends in to meet you. So you'd get to know people and start feeling comfortable right away."

"Oh. But I thought—"

"Thought what?"

"I thought we'd—you know—" I didn't know exactly what I thought. But I knew it involved only Maisie and me, and not a bunch of other people.

She giggled. "You're too tired to string two thoughts together. I'll let you get a bath and some rest. I'll wake you in time for dinner."

"Okay." I felt the lump in my pocket. "Wait! I almost forgot. I brought you something."

Proudly I produced the glorious marble and held it toward her. She took it and rolled it over in her hand.

"Thank you. It's pretty."

"Feel how heavy it is," I urged. "It's a top-notch shooter. Sammy Wardlow's pride and joy, until I made him fork it over. Boy, was he ever steamed when I yelled 'keepsies'!"

I waited for her to congratulate me. She looked at me as if I were speaking Swahili.

I sucked in a breath. "Anyway, I knew you'd like it."

"I do." She turned it so it sparkled. "It's a beaut. I'll keep it right here on the dresser, where it will catch the light."

Catch the light? "It's—it's for playing with." Did I really have to explain?

She shot me a sidelong glance. "At our high school, only boys play with marbles."

My face grew hot. "Oh, piffle. What do the girls do?"

"This and that." She gave a little shrug. "Play cribbage, mostly. And talk about the boys."

I stared at her, unsure of what to say. Disappointment washed over me. This was going to be one long summer, if all we could do was play cribbage and talk about boys.

She set the marble next to a framed photo.

"Who's that?" I pointed.

Maisie blushed. "That's Herbert."

Sensing we were entering strange and unfamiliar territory, I proceeded with caution.

"Who's he?"

Her color deepened. "A boy at school. I think he's the bee's knees, but he never even notices me. As far as he's concerned, I blend with the wallpaper."

"Then he's a dope." A good-looking dope, I had to admit. Although his ears stuck out a little.

"You have your rest now," she said quickly. "You'll find clean towels next to the tub."

Too flagged to argue, I soaked in the immaculate claw-footed tub, put on fresh underthings, and crawled into Maisie's bed.

When I awoke, dazed and disoriented, the setting sun slanted through the window.

"Get out of bed, sleepyhead." Maisie chirped as she set a tray on the nightstand. "You were sleeping so soundly that Mother didn't want to disturb you for dinner. She sent up a sandwich and a glass of milk instead. But now you'd better get changed. Our guests will be arriving any minute."

I sat up and nibbled the ham sandwich while Maisie bustled around the room, chatting about this or that person who'd be at the party.

"Margaret's father works with Dad at the mill. She lives three doors down."

"Will Sir Herbert the Sublime be there?"

"Yes, but you mustn't let on that I like him. I'd be mortified."

"Mum's the word." I noticed she'd changed into a sophisticated lilac-colored sheath decorated with beaded swirls, and a matching headband worn low across her forehead. I sighed at the thought of my yellow daisy dress, in all its Midwestern earnestness. But after I was dressed, she pinned my hair in a way that made it look bobbed, if you didn't peer too closely. She also lent me a bit of lip rouge. I smiled at the mirror. What Frances didn't know wouldn't hurt her.

Downstairs the doorbell rang. "Let's get a wiggle on," Maisie said, and off we went.

The next couple hours passed in a blur. We sipped punch, and Maisie introduced me around. When the dancing started, I mostly stood by, changing records on the Victrola and watching Maisie turkey-trot with one fellow after another, none of whom was Herbert. What was the matter with that goof? Couldn't he see Maisie was the cat's meow?

Finally, bored and feeling like a canceled stamp, I escaped the muggy parlor and wandered out to the porch. Moonlight spilled over the lawn and glittered on Lake Coeur d'Alene. I breathed in the refreshing pine-scented air.

At one end of the porch, under an electric light, a group of boys knelt in a circle, playing marbles. Suddenly my shooting finger itched. I walked over to them.

"Hey, can I play?"

The boys glanced up. Herbert said, "Girls don't play marbles."

"Malarkey. Says who?"

"Aw, let her in," said a boy named Stanley. "She'll probably fizzle out, anyway."

I gathered my skirt and knelt on the plank floor. Stanley lined up a few aggies from his stash and I knuckled down. "We're playing for fair, not for keeps," he said solemnly. I nodded.

After several games in which I'd held my own, a shadow hovered. Glancing over, I recognized Maisie's dancing slippers.

"There you are," she said, hands on hips. "I wondered where you went."

Then she must have noticed Herbert, because her breath caught and fluttered a little. He didn't glance up. I sighed. Clearly my help was needed.

"Maisie," I said, with a meaningful look, "why don't you go upstairs and fetch the *present* I gave you?" I hoped she'd take the hint. If Herbert wouldn't dance with the girl, the least he could do was let her shoot.

She hesitated, but left and came back, carrying the blue cats-eye, along with a leather pouch full of mibs that must have been tucked away somewhere with other childhood relics.

"Make room." She joined us on the floor.

Herbert's eyes widened when he saw the gleaming cat's-eye. They grew even wider as she handily won game after game.

I grinned. The old Maisie was back.

Later, when I spotted her and Herbert fox-trotting together, my heart sang that a talent for shooting marbles could succeed where lip rouge failed.

I wandered across the dark lawn and found a bench facing toward Lake Coeur d'Alene. Moonlight rippled on the water.

The boy called Stanley appeared out of nowhere.

"May I join you?"

"It's a free country." I shifted over. He folded his lanky body onto the bench, careful not to spill a dish containing a heaping concoction of ice cream, chocolate syrup, and nuts.

"Want some?"

"No, thanks."

We sat in silence for a moment. Then he said, "Gosh, I never met a girl who was good at marbles before."

"Maisie's a whiz," I agreed.

"I meant you."

"Oh."

He cleared his throat. "A bunch of us are going swimming tomorrow. You and Maisie should come." It was more a statement than a question.

"Oh," I said again.

It was going to be a long summer if all I could think of to say was "oh."

He lifted a spoonful of ice cream, held it toward me, and smiled.

Maybe this summer wasn't going to be such a dud, after all.

That House There by the Lake

By Emily Moore

What has happened in that place,
That house there by the lake?
Weary, powerful people
Lumbering.
Their families enjoying its space,
its design,
its wealth.
One after another,
They attempted to keep the mill alive.
The house became a vacation home,
A public gift.

What is happening in that place,
That house there by the lake?
Inspired, immersed people,
Indulging
With companions in their yoga,
Their writings,
Their parties.
Month after month,
They fill its current history with life
The house offers old beauty,
A treasured view.

What will happen to that place,
That house there by the lake?
Positive, proactive people
Preserving.
Their comrades fighting against time,
The decay,
The indifference.
Year after year,
We'll tell the world of its worth.
The house has stood a century,
And will last for many more.

Jewett House Josephine

by Josephie Jackson

Hullo dear friend,

I have decided right from the start to give this letter a title, much like a memo: "Welcome Home."

It has been such a while since I wrote to you, and please, do forgive me as you know how it is to settle into somewhere new. Finally, I have a decent chunk of time that I can spend putting some thoughts on paper to share with you, and I do know you have been busy with life too, and look forward to hearing you share some of your gem moments since I moved away. Those short blips of texts we have gotten into the dreadful, but convenient, habit of using remind me of black holes, totally absorbed in themselves, burping out a radio wave now and then to let the universe know they are there, somewhere; a "here I am! Come and find me" call of hide and seek and no one really searching and finding anymore, just playing tag with short call outs.

It really is remarkable how much time it takes. Time to grow new roots, movements and memories, even to learn to navigate a new space. It takes more energy than one would assume it would. I have given up obsessing about how many boxes remain unpacked.

Our rambling letters, like those fast-paced, pinging conversations when we would send ideas sparking and ping-ponging down rabbit holes, are something I miss very much, so I hope your time is starting to free up, too, so we may resume those adventures, at least on paper.

Regarding the 'title,' I needed a little time to share something that I have found to be almost unsettling to hear. It is a simple two-word phrase that has been said to me here, since moving to Coeur d'Alene, more than once. Although said with the utmost kindness, it almost sends me reeling each time. The sound of it, like two rocks dropping, one after the other, into a vastly deep and dark well, and finally making a sound in the void of something I did not know I had even been listening for, an echo of a place, a space to set roots and be irrigated by this very water, and for the first time ever, in my life, to hear… "welcome home."

The day we closed on our place here was the first time I have ever heard, "welcome home" as its recipient. It was said by our Real Estate Agent in a tone that seemed to be a proclamation that this statement was really what made the closing official. And, it has not been the last I heard it said. When changing the car title to Idaho at the local county office, the chap there said the same thing, "welcome home," and at the local stores where those cheerful and chatty checkout staff, ubiquitous to "CdA", have more than once, in asking their well-meaning queries about my accent and story to here, said the same thing, "welcome home."

How peculiar it feels to hear this.

You may have read that recent study which examined how change, even good change, is a stressor and takes time (and gobs of self-kindness) to adjust well to, and at the same time it is so good for the brain to learn new things. Sounds like moving is like exercising and school all wrapped into one experience, don't you think? This move, although good, is one that gobbles up time like a growing child.

Well, I have been exploring a little about here, although not as much as I would like, since we last touched base, however, this place is quietly roaring with potential. It also has the funniest 'gate keepers' of citizens and now I must admit that I am just as guilty of using a quaint expression of vanity, guised as both modest and protective.

"What on earth are you talking about?" I hear you say. Well, it is like this, there is *another* 'Coeur d'Alene expression,' which usually goes like this, "don't tell anyone how beautiful it is here!"

Anyway, to try and staunch the influx of newcomers, the locals use with great futility this phrase which, of course, does quite the opposite. Like juicy gossip and noxious weeds, news of this delightful place seems to spread like the Big Burn wildfire hereabouts of 1910.

Summer residents are, honestly, considered somewhat faux residents by those who happily winter in Coeur d'Alene, and you will be asked with suspicion, "do you winter?" (another expression), and if you reply, "yes, of course!" you are viewed as being somewhat 'legitimate'… for a new resident. Of course, to add further childlike 'proof' I throw out that I also have found my own wild huckleberries. Despite the rumor this proves you have finally made 'native status,' it does not hold as much weight as hoped for.

It was this last winter, my second, that I was introduced to an historic house that is special to Coeur d'Alene and it seemed immediately to be such a lovely example of both the "welcome home" and "shhh! Don't tell anyone how lovely it is here" memes.

It sits tucked about halfway between Tubbs Hill and the satellite of the 14th hole at the Resort Golf Club, at the end of a delightful and small stretch of a proper sandy beach, as though shy or a bit reserved, a quietly understated, almost grand house. You really do not hear much about this house although it is in the tourist literature. For the most part it is overlooked (thankfully), being off the 'main drag,' so to speak. But it is special in its firm and understated way and reminds me of so much of the character of Coeur d'Alene and perhaps even this remarkable country at large I now live in.

Here, in Coeur d'Alene, the locals breathe a sigh of relief when the summer folk have gone, although they are most fond of them, there is a tangible change and in the stores and on quieter streets, people nod to each other in open recognition, as though we had been together on the St Crispin's Day battlefield, a band of brothers, of 'stayers'. The pretense is gone, if you will. There is a belief that it was those cautionary and often exaggerated tales of epic winters that has both people and boats packed up, to be brought out again after snow melt; leaving the magic of cheap, uncluttered ski slopes and quiet, snow padded forests to "us" who call this place home year-round. The image of parents flopping into a comfy sofa with an exhausted "whew!" after their much loved but exhausting children have finally fallen asleep, is not far off the mark.

The old part of Coeur d'Alene, right on and about the lakeshore, where The House is, reminds of a lakeside version of Carmel… with its similar quaint and various architecture with homes perfectly coiffed by exquisite gardens in the long summer days. In that 'Carmel by the Lake' (as I call it) neighborhood on the way to 'The House' on my first visit to it, I passed a little hilly residential street with a sign that proudly declared, "Caution Sledding Hill". Caution?! How about 'Celebrate'?!

What a perfect Norman Rockwell image it made regarding childhood. I fell in love with the place a little bit more when I saw that sign and what it meant. To this foreigner, it was so perfectly quaint and delightful for many reasons. Driving a little further down from the "Caution Sledding Hill" sign, past Tubbs Hill and the park on 10th Street, I followed the road that lies alongside the afore mentioned beach. It is divided into both public and private areas. As I drove in one private section, there was another happy sight. A small crowd of brightly colored beach chairs, still sunning in Stirling grey light, tucked into the snow up to their armrests and facing the show happening out upon the lake.

The lake was a frosted silver platter, merging flawlessly into the trout shimmer of sky as backdrop, the stage for a lithe chorus line of vestal mist sprites, rising now and then to a 100-feet; swooping down to gather foggy skirts before reaching and twirling and swirling into ethereal dancing tornadoes, a sight only equal to the primordial fascination of watching twirls of flame in a fireplace or campfire; here was a sight that summer folk shall never see.

And this house, The House, had prime viewing from its front rooms and generous porch. This porch that has seen many performances of many kinds.

As you enter this house, it is peculiar, just like the "welcome home" statement, it is odd because it is much like realizing your hand feels small, yet safe, when held by a large and warm handshake; this house conveys both 'welcome' and that it is still a 'home'.

You feel secure in its solid and sensible "four square" style that was an American architectural Revolution to counter and tidy up the frilly Victorian style. Airy yet protective, simplified and functional yet attractive; with tall enough ceilings to enable high thoughts to flourish, not mean and squatty low ceilings that feel like a pulled down hat brim on the soul, where your hands could reach out and touch the roof, and where thoughts don't go much higher.

Home. This was a home, built between 1915 and 1917, times of great changes that defined another era that the 'wash, rinse, repeat' of history does before putting it all together a little differently to trick the unaware. There was a global conflict and epidemics, great leaps in science, medicine and technology, air power used in novel ways, Einstein was rocking the intellectual world, lifespans were getting longer and hems were getting shorter and women were showing leg and 'kicking butt,' and Sears was the Amazon Prime of the time, distributing along vast railroad highways nearly everything a person could want, even the blueprints and all the building materials, if needed, for other 'four square' homes for this developing country.

Just as the corridor between Coeur d'Alene and Spokane is filling in today, tracts of land were being fleshed out along these rail arteries as precursors to modern day suburbs with sturdy, Prairie style inspired 'four squares', that even Frank Lloyd Wright adopted and morphed into his own.

All peaceful times and all healing times in history belong to the epicenter of the home of the average citizen, where children grow on a balanced diet of self-control and exploration, self-responsibility and self-regard, tolerant encouragement and boundaries without rigidity, a kindly taught stoicism and kindly heard questions, where to spell love, as children do, with "t.i.m.e.," is safe and abundant, especially time for themselves, in the safe walls and house yards, and neighborhoods; raised with expectations of reaching potential with practiced self-sufficiency which flows like the St. Joe River into this lake of deep and quiet abundance and flows out further to benefit greater still down the Spokane River; too busy to rule or be ruled by others, by human interpreted doctrine, creed or common mandate. "Caution. Sledding Hill."

The house still patiently overlooks change, even the influx of new comers clogging up roads, haughty philosophies, unchanged, brought in from failed states, ugly horn blowing, smothering with impersonal distance, it is the genuine charm of locals, who are happier in their own skins than the most affluent newbie, that portray the comfortable air of this house. I hope the 'welcome' associated with Coeur d'Alene will endure as that is what, in great part, helps define a home.

There is so much to catch up on, dear friend, and so I do hope you shall come and visit us as soon as you are able to get away. There are so many beautiful places here about including the claimed 'Center of the Universe' down the road in Wallace, and so many memories to be made that I want to share with you, but please, promise me, *do not* to tell anyone how wonderful it is here.

If you come in winter, we can see if the mist sprites of the lake can call out as we watch, tucked snugly under the arms of the porch of The House, so you can hear for yourself the secret call of Coeur d'Alene, "welcome home".

The Parlor Window

by Terry Robinson

from the water's edge
her window seems in proportion;
sitting in the parlor it feels much larger,
a cinematic experience

green mountain forests, blue sky, turquoise lake
framed perfectly
like a painting, or
a motion picture

flow of activity continually changing
high-powered boat races
followed in a few minutes
by a graceful sailing yacht

one in a hurry
to go nowhere
the other
enjoying the journey

if only the parlor had a voice
what would she say?
the mysteries she could expose!
from one hundred years ago

the steamships of the early nineteen hundreds
passing by on the way to where?
did Captain Sorensen of the Amelia Wheaton visit
or sound the ship's horn?

how did Huntington Taylor feel giving up his home
to the new Rutledge Mill manager?
whom ultimately the house would be named after
and what of the Weyerhaeuser family connection?

and does it really matter, so long as we have the pleasure
of watching life through her window?

Elsie's Story

by Anna Goodwin

My name is Elsie Owens and I remember Coeur d'Alene, Idaho well. It was the summer of 1918 and I was seventeen years old. You say, "Elsie, you can't still be alive. You'd be one hundred and sixteen!"

And I'd say, "You are absolutely right." I died thirty-five years ago. But I am not a ghost. I am a memory.

When I heard that the Jewett House was a hundred years old this year, I decided to come to check out my old "stomping grounds." After all, this is the place where my life changed forever.

Actually, to understand my story you'll need to know a little background history. First of all, America was at war with Germany. Second, Coeur d'Alene in those days was a mining and lumbering town of about 7,500 people in 1900. Due to the loss of a million acres of standing forest in Montana, Idaho, and Eastern Washington during the great fire, often called the Big Burn of 1910, the population decreased to 6,000. The lumber industry was in trouble. The other historical fact often forgotten is that much of the world, including America, was engulfed by the Flu Pandemic of 1917-1920. Millions of people died.

Now to my story: My family, as were most families in our area of New York City, was neither rich nor poor. We lived in a small and modest home. No doubt you would have called us an ordinary, happy family. My father worked as an accountant at a millinery business and my mother raised my younger brother, my little sister, and me in the ways of her old English and Protestant traditions. Our parents protected us from everything, even bad news in the paper that might disturb us. So I knew little about what was happening in the rest of the world, never mind this country.

The boys at school often whistled at me and called out, "Hey, gorgeous," but who would trust those boys anyway? Yes, I had long blonde hair, and girls with blonde hair are supposed to have more fun, right? Not in my family. My mom and dad were very strict.

And then one day, within hours, my world shattered.

Through the front window I saw my father stagger up the outside steps of the house and bang at the wooden door. I ran to answer it. As I yanked it open he stumbled and collapsed onto the floor, gasping and coughing. His face was red and puffy. When I touched it, my hand burned as though I had picked up hot coal in our fireplace. His body began to jerk. My heart pounded and I yelled for my mother. "Mom, Mom! It's Dad. He's dying!"

She raced down the stairs and dropped down on her knees beside him. I heard her whisper, "God help us. It's the influenza." Two days later, he was gone. Three weeks later, my thirteen-year-old brother, Joseph, died. Every day we heard of more people who were sick and dying. At last our minister called on us and soon after, my mother left to take care of a family in the parish. My sister and I were alone. I would often sit and stare out the window wondering who would be next. Would it be me? Would it be my mother? Or my six-year-old sister, Nellie? Then one night the minister, face strained and white, came to our house with news. He said, "We will take care of everything."

My mother never returned.

The rest, as they say, "is history." I have no idea how many days, weeks, Nellie and I hid out in the house. One day I heard a loud bang on the front door and when I opened it just a crack, a disheveled older man shoved a letter through it. "Sorry, Ma'am," he said. "This house now belongs to the bank."

I fell to my knees. For the first time since my father's death, I buried my face in my hands and sobbed. Nellie raced to me and begged, "Elsie, Elsie. We have no home. Don't let us die!" I wiped my tears, then hers, straightened, and held my head high. With a forced smile, I said, "It's okay. Don't worry. I'll take care of us. We need to leave."

"But where to? There's no one here that will help us."

She was right. Our parents' families still lived in England. And our friends were sick or in crisis, just like we were.

That night I tossed and turned. I was desperate. I had to get Nellie out of there and find work in a safe place. Finally I knelt by my bed and prayed. "Dear Jesus, please let me know what to do." Out of the blue I remembered that some time ago, my father and his friend had talked about Idaho and Washington. Men, and even families, were flocking west to work in the mines and lumber mills. Yes! I could take Nellie and find work far away from New York.

I grabbed a suitcase from under my bed and rushed around the house, filling it with anything Nellie and I might need—clothes, any valuables I could trade for what we would need like mom's silverware, even soap, candles, matches, and cheese and bread. I emptied the quarters, dimes and pennies from the cracked jar in the kitchen into a woolen mitten and tied it with a pink bow from Nellie's favorite doll. I stopped and looked at the doll. Should I bring it? There wasn't much room. But Nellie... Finally I shoved the doll into the suitcase next to Nellie's clothes.

Then I scrounged around my parent's bedroom and found the cash my dad always hid under the floorboards near the head of the bed. In one of the dresser drawers I found a picture of the whole family playing at the ocean. Tears stung my eyes. I took it and located mom's little wooden jewelry box. When I opened it, I saw my mom's pearl necklace and earrings from my dad and my parents' wedding rings. I took the jewelry and placed it into one of my mother's lace handkerchiefs and tied it.

That morning we dressed in our very best dresses and we ate some toast and cooked oatmeal—no milk, no sugar. As usual, Nellie screamed as I brushed her long golden hair. We pulled on our coats and hats. I grabbed the suitcase and Nellie's hand and we hurried out onto the street.

You ask, "Weren't you scared? Didn't you want to go back?"

Of course I was scared. Who wouldn't be? But no. I never looked back. Not even for a moment...at least not until later.

At the railroad station I bought tickets to Seattle. Surely there would be a place somewhere on the trip for us to stay. Five days later we pulled into a station. It said "Coeur d'Alene." Strange name, I thought. I'm never getting off here. But when Nellie heard a woman call out, "Fresh molasses cookies for sale," she rushed to the window. "Elsie. Elsie. Can we get a cookie? Please. Please."

I grabbed our suitcase, Nellie's hand, and her doll and ran off the train toward the now retreating woman. When we caught up with her I pulled out the little mitten and counted out the pennies. We snatched the cookies and dashed toward the train. Too late. We were just in time to see it round the bend ahead of us.

So now? Now what? Dejected, Nellie and I sat down on a wooden bench near the entrance of the train station and munched our cookies. I had to find a job, and quick. But where?

Just then a young woman about my height but with high heels, fur coat, and diamond earrings stepped out of the train station next to us, holding a baby in her arms. As she let the door slam, she tripped on the cement stair and began to tumble. I grabbed the baby out of her arms as she fell to her knees. The baby began to scream. Trembling, the woman got up, her face white as my mother's bleached sheets. "Thank you Miss. Thank you so much. You saved my Lisa. How can I ever repay you?"

I handed her the baby, and before I could think I said, "I need a job."

"Heavens to Betsy," she said and laughed. "What are you doing here?" When I explained, she said, "Yes, of course. I'll hire you to take care of Lisa. My husband, Henry, and I will be staying with our friends, the Taylors, for the month. Huntington Taylor is the manager of the Edward Rutledge Timber Company here and has a giant house on the lake. They are kind people. I'm sure they'd understand."

And that's how I got to the Jewett House. (It wasn't called that at the time.) Wow! What an incredible home—at least four times as big as the house I had grown up in, with a giant parlor, a two-sided fireplace, a piano, and plush sofas. The dining room was big enough to seat twenty people or more.

But you still don't know how my life changed forever at this place. So here goes:

Not long after I started working for Henry and Judy Russell, a new family came to stay at the Taylors': a mom, a dad, and a tall, very handsome young man in uniform. Each day he sat on the large wooden porch at the front of the house and stared into the lake ahead of him. And each day, as I took Lisa and Nellie out to play, I would say "good morning" to him. His face appeared dour and drawn and he said nothing. Sometimes I noticed him looking at me, but he glanced away as soon as he saw me look back. The strange thing was that his parents **always** remained nearby.

Seeing him so sad hurt my heart. I wished I could help him. At last I asked Mrs. Russell, "Ma'am, who is he?"

"The parents are close friends of the Taylors. They own a lumber company too." She lowered her eyes. "Eric came home from the war and he hasn't been right since. They thought the silence here and the lake would do him good."

"What's wrong with him?" I whispered.

She looked into my eyes, her voice breaking. "They say he saw too much in the war. Do you understand?"

I nodded my head. Oh, yes, I understood. I, too, had seen too much.

Two days later at dusk I sat on the beach and watched the waves splash onto the sand. I tried not to think about New York and my mom and dad, but I couldn't stop my thoughts. The memories flooded back, and all I wanted to do was to reverse time and wash away the last month with the waves. I longed to be happy again.

In the growing darkness I saw the young man in uniform, Eric, walk onto the beach. I sat very still, hoping he wouldn't see me. Slowly he took off his shoes, then his uniform. He folded each piece of his clothing neatly, and placed it in a pile on the beach. On top of the pile he dropped what you call his "dog tags." He stopped for a while with his hands stretched out as though blessing the uniform and the place, then headed into the waves and swam away.

I watched him for a short while, thinking he was going for a nice evening swim. Suddenly I saw bubbles rise to the surface, but no Eric! Oh, no, what was he doing? I threw off my sweater, skirt, and shoes and, wearing only my camisole and bloomers, I ran into the lake. I was a strong swimmer. I could save him! I reached him and tugged at him willing him to surface and breathe. But he struggled to get away from me until I was so exhausted I had to let go. As though in a nightmare, I felt myself sinking, sinking, sinking. Then nothing.

The next thing I remember was someone shaking me. He shouted. "Come back here, Elsie. Don't you dare die on me!" I sputtered and coughed. When I opened my eyes, I stared into Eric's face, his arms holding me tight, shaking me, his wet, dark curly hair plastered to his head. "Thank God you're okay." He held me that way for what seemed like at least an hour.

And that's when my life changed forever. And so did his. Six months later, two days after my eighteenth birthday, and five days before Christmas, Eric and I were married. Guess where? At the house you call the Jewett House. Now couples love to have their weddings here. Isn't that amazing? Maybe we had a premonition about the future. Or maybe we made the future happen.

Eric joined his father's lumber business and we settled down in Coeur d'Alene. We had three children, and of course Nellie lived with us until she got married. Eric went on frequent rescue missions when someone was lost or in trouble, and I took in children that parents were unable to take care of for a while.

Often Eric and I would spent hours together on the beach, holding each other and talking about what had happened in the past that made us so sad. Slowly our sadness changed to joy. We had a purpose—a reason to live. Sure, we had our problems, but we both worked together to learn from them and move on. People asked us, "What made the difference? How come you could heal together when you couldn't do it alone?" My answer was then, and is still the same, "Love and total acceptance. And time."

My dear readers, in those many years we were married, we truly learned love so much greater than earthly love. And now we are together forever. Here at the Jewett House we are merely a memory...a memory of love that still walks the halls and the grounds. People who come here often say this is a place they can feel safe, feel at peace, and heal, just like Eric and I did in 1918 when the house was merely a year old.

The 1916 – 1917 Summer Serenade

by Larry Telles

The sawing, hammering, and sawdust were gone. The majestic house with the sprawling porch by the lake was done. Wicker chairs and a petite table were placed sparsely on the wooden floor. Directly behind, the oak door concealed the ornate screen door. Walking or riding by the house, a lilting melody emanated from the large horn connected to a gramophone. It was summer 1917 and there was music filling the cloudless sky. A potpourri of musical patterns filled the small currents of air all afternoon, and every afternoon. The proud owners of the house by the lake had a collection of the 1916 and 1917 hit songs of the day and they let the city hear them.

Released	Song Title	Artist	Record Label
02/1916	Beatrice Fairfax, Tell me What to Do?	Ada Jones	Victor #17926
02/1916	M-O-T-H-E-R (A word that means the world to me)	Henry Burr	Victor #17913
03/1916	The Old Folks at Home	Taylor Trio	Columbia #1915
05/1916	St. Louis Blues	Prince's Orchestra	Columbia #5772
05/1916	There's a Broken Heart for Every Light on Broadway	Else Baker	Victor #17943
06/1916	My Old Kentucky Home	Alma Gluck	Victor #74468
06/1916	O Solo Mio	Enrico Caruso	Victor #87249
07/1916	The Missouri Waltz	Victor Military Band	Victor #18026
07/1916	Where did Robinson Crusoe go With Friday on Saturday Night?	Al Jolson	Columbia #1976
08/1916	Down Where the Swannee River Flows	Al Jolson	Columbia #2007
09/1916	If I knocked the 'L' out of Kelly (I would still be Kelly to me)	Marguerite Farrell	Columbia #39998
10/1916	Oh how she could Yacki Hacki Wicki Wachi Woo (That's Love in Honolulu).	Authur Collins	Victor #18110
10/1916	Pretty Baby	Billy Murray	Victor #17945
11/1916	There's a Little Bit of Bad in Every Good Little Girl	Billy Murray	Victor #18143
11/1916	Santa Lucia	Enrico Caruso	Victor #88560
12/1916	I'm Gonna Make Hay While the Sun Shines in Virginia	Marion Harris	Victor #18143
12/1916	I'll Take You Home Again Kathleen	Walter Van Brunt	Edison #80160
12/1916	The Sunshine of Your Smile	John McCormack	Victor #64622

Date	Title	Artist	Label
01/1917	Somebody May be there While I'm Gone	Al Jolson	Columbia 2124
01/1917	O'Brien is Tryin' to Speak Hawaiian	Horace Wright	Victor #18167
02/1917	Poor Butterfly	Victor Military Band	Victor #35605
02/1917	They're Wearing Em Higher in Hawaii	Arthur Collins	Victor #18210
03/1917	Hush-a-Bye My Baby (Missouri Waltz)	Elsie Baker	Victor #18214
04/1917	Pack up Your Troubles in Your Old Kit Bag	Knickerbocker Quartet	Columbia 2181
05/1917	For Me and My Gal	Van and Schenek	Victor #18258
05/1917	The Star-Spangled Banner	John McCormack	Victor #64664
06/1917	Oh Johnny, Oh Johnny, Oh!	American Quartet	Victor #18279
06/1917	M-I-S-S-I-S-S-I-P-P-I	Anna Wheaton	Columbia 2224
07/1917	Lookout Mountain	Henry Burr	Victor #18295
08/1917	Till the Clouds Roll By	Anna Wheaton	Columbia 2261
09/1917	Over There	American Quartet	Victor #18333
09/1917	There's a Long, Long Trail A-Winding	John McCormack	Victor #64694
09/1917	Good Bye Broadway, Hello France	American Quartet	Victor #18335
09/1917	The Old Grey Mare	Prince's Orchestra	Columbia 2285
10/1917	Darktown Strutter's Ball	Dixieland Jazz Band	Columbia 2297
12/1917	Send Me Away with a Smile	John McCormack	Victor #64741

All of this music is available to be seen and heard on You Tube.

From the Legend of Blackjack Diamond

An excerpt from "The Welcomed Warriors Return"
PREPARATION

by Jesse Warburton

It's Friday, the day before his fight, and Jackson had hinted to Taylor that he likes to spend most of the day to himself. Pop knows it's not a day of any serious training and he's been through this with Jackson many times. He lets Blackjack plan his day: going on long walks; perhaps a swim in the lake or a conversation with some very old trees; when he sees any wildlife, deer, or raccoon, sometimes even squirrels, he likes to sing to them his favorite Gospel songs. And while he's been told he doesn't have a very good voice, his audience has never complained. They just peer at him curiously. He talks to his mother and his father, too, though they are hundreds of miles away; and speaks to his Comanche grandfather and others who have passed on into the spirit world. But mostly, he talks to his Eternal Father and Jesus.

Distractions and activities that have taken him from this ideal have troubled him in the past. He doesn't want to appear ungrateful to his hosts, the Huntington family, so he asked Pop if he would speak to Taylor about his hopes of how the 'day before his fight' unfolds.

Jackson finds a thick forest setting with a grassy meadow. He's wearing the leather shirt given to him by his mother's brother, Jack Rabbit Moonrise. It brings our warrior into deep, deep thoughts of the previous weekend.

Jack Rabbit was one of his Ma's family that he found easy to relate to. He's not a boxer, but he is a legendary wrestler, Indian style. They had a chance to talk about Jackson's mother, and Jack Rabbit told of the special 'little sister' that she was and how she would often disappear as a child for days and then reappear as if nothing had happened. Jack said any kind of punishment was useless, so they simply accepted her peculiar nature and let her wander off and return as she pleased. They could never get her to reveal where she would go or what she did in the days she was gone. She did this from about the time she was six years old. She would only say that she was 'with friends'.

These thoughts and many of the impressions he gained when his Kalispell relatives visited him the previous weekend were all rolling through his mind as he sat himself down in the meadow near a small creek. He sang songs he knew from church and prayed vocally, at times expressing his hope for forgiveness for the weaknesses he feels he has. He stayed in this special secluded place until late in the afternoon. After a peaceful sleep, he opened his eyes to see a deer just a few feet away drinking from the creek. When Jackson began to raise himself up the deer calmly wandered away. Hunger was getting the best of him so he decided he would find his way back to the Huntington home.

He knew his way back and normally he would keep to animal trails and read the signs of what creatures preceded him on these paths. But today, for whatever reason, he chose to walk alongside the road, the main road back to Coeur d'Alene, it turned out to be.

He heard a vehicle approaching from behind. It was a truck with five young men, wearing work clothes. They slowed down, and seeing Blackjack wearing the leather shirt and moccasins, they all began to taunt him, "Injun boy, go back to the reservation" and "We don't need no Redskins around here," and other debasing words. Their truck stopped about twenty yards away, as if waiting for him. Jackson had just left a beautiful, peaceful place where he had melted into a meadow, feeling he was being held in his Father's arms. Now, he was back in the real world of hate and prejudice. He heard an inner voice whisper, "You can outrun them through the forest…or, if you wish, you can fight them."

Jackson felt a need to preserve himself for his fight the next day. Five against one can be a gamble, a risk he didn't want to take today. He bolted into the forest and felt confident he could outrun them if they decided to pursue him. They did pursue him, making one critical mistake. They began to yell, "Yellow redskin", "Chicken-shit, Injun boy" "Why are you runnin', scaredee cat."

Jackson slowed his pace. He knew they would not likely all reach him at one time. And the forest was getting thicker and it was always his friend. He pretended to stumble, and the fastest of his pursuers was right upon him. He was kneeling as 'attacker number one' lunged toward him. He rewarded him with a powerful strike to his chest and he went rolling to the ground, writhing in pain. One down, four to go.

Jackson resumed his slow-paced run, checking back to see if he would be met by one or two or more. Two of them were in close pursuit. He remembered his uncle Jack Rabbit had shown him an interesting wrestling move the previous weekend when they met. It was a throw that would use his attacker's momentum against himself.

He passed a large tree that whispered, "Use me" and he again pretended to stumble, turning just in time to grab 'number two' by the arms, and in a twisting motion heaved him into the tree head first. "Thank you" he whispered to the tree, turning to 'number three' who seemed alarmed to see his friend falling to the ground, screaming in pain. He instantly decided he didn't want to be there, but before he could do anything about it, Jackson was on him with three successive blows, one to the center of his chest, momentarily depriving him of his breathing and two to his face, his nose issuing blood. Three down, two to go. Maybe not.

The last two of the five had stopped a short distance away and watched their buddies go down. They decided they wanted no part of this 'Redskin coward'. They ran much faster toward the road than they did chasing Jackson. Perhaps what they saw happening ahead of them tended to stifle their eagerness to catch up to their Injun victim.

Blackjack did not follow them. He felt they had learned a lesson they wouldn't forget any time soon. Perhaps 'numbers one, two and three' had not been so lucky in being the fastest of the five. Fast or bold, whichever. The lessons they received would take a couple of days to sink in; probably, sooner than their wounds would heal. Would it change them? Probably not. But it might just cause them to pause before they decide to chase someone into a forest again; especially, if that someone is wearing an Indian shirt and moccasins.

Jackson didn't receive any injury whatsoever, so he realized no one would know of this encounter unless he told them. He really didn't want to talk about it, and explaining what happened would seem too much like bragging, so he decided no one needed to know. There was a slight rip in his leather shirt, but he could simply say he was running in the forest, which of course was true. He had known for many years that talking about bad things that happen can give them power to move further, keeping them alive and affecting others in bad ways. He hoped he wouldn't even think much about it himself. And he didn't want to take any of this experience into the ring tomorrow afternoon.

Fletcher "Gunboat" O'Reilly may be an opponent that Blackjack needed to beat on, but he was not someone he would send face first into a large tree. He respected O'Reilly; Jackson had no respect for those who called him a coward and cursed his Indian blood. He did feel that he learned something though, through this altercation: the wrestling move his uncle Jack Rabbit showed him really worked;

and while he'd been talking to trees for many years (and hearing their whisperings), he couldn't remember when a tree has been his friend in a fight before. He pauses to thank his Eternal Father for letting his kindred spirits speak to him in the forest and guide his every move. He asks his Father that perhaps those unfortunate ones who caught up to him, will have a 'change of heart' once they recover from their injuries. Jackson always seems to hope for the best in people.

"Blackjack, wake up. Aren't we gonna run today? It's Saturday and you gotta fight today. Don't'cha think we better run?" It's Saturday morning and Jackson had thought of maybe skipping his early morning run, which he sometimes does on fight day. But Richard, Huntington Taylor's twelve-year-old son, didn't get the word about Jackson liking to keep to himself before his fight. Richard missed seeing Jackson yesterday and he's excited that the day everyone has been waiting for has finally arrived.

"Well, ah…I ah, sure, let's go run." He could do without running one day, but he could tell Richard would be somewhat let down if they didn't do their usual jog together along the lake shore. "We won't need a long run today, but a short one will be good. Oh, is this the day I fight O'Reilly?"

"Yea, didn't you remember, today's Saturday. You gotta fight today." Richard sees a slight curl of a smile on Jackson and realizes he's been goofed with. "You're Joshin' me. You knew this was that day. You're just kidden' me, I know it."

Jackson's happy that the first person he sees today is Richard. He's a kid at heart himself, and in his world of boxing, kids don't play a big role. It's a world of bragging and betting, smoky gyms, and late-night gambling. It's a part of his life that he has gotten used to, but he's never really been comfortable in that world.

"Beat'cha to the beach!" Jackson bolts off from the porch where he's been sleeping this past week. Richard is in close pursuit. "Last one in the water is a pig's butt!" As they race to the lake, Jackson pretends to slip and fall, letting Richard get to the lake first. Richard jumps in, turns, and yells, "You're a pig's butt, I win."

Jackson knows the water's cold and Richard usually doesn't go for cold water until they've heated up from running, especially early in the morning. Our warrior doesn't get in the water, but smiles at Richard, "I may be a pig's butt, but I'm dry and you're cold and wet." He lets out a big laugh, "I'm goin' runnin'" and heads down the shoreline. Richard, now figuring he's been goofed with again, leaves the cold lake and follows his favorite teacher. He's knows the lessons he learns from Blackjack are from his heart, and always in fun.

"I'm gonna get back at you one of these days, Blackjack. You just wait and see." And Jackson knows he will.

From the Legend of Blackjack Diamond

An excerpt from "The Welcomed Warriors Return"
REDEMPTION

by Jesse Warburton

As the fight day unfolds, Blackjack and Pop make the rounds over to the high school and survey the situation; the ring, the ropes, and the weather. Outdoor boxing matches have always depended on good weather. Rainy weather changes everything. If the fight is not cancelled, a slippery canvas or rain in the eyes can influence the outcome of the fight. Not to mention how it is to the spectators. Today, it's somewhat cloudy, but no rain is expected. At least the clouds don't look too ominous. And it's not a blistering, hot day.

People are arriving in Coeur d'Alene from all directions. Some arrived yesterday, with the saloons and taverns busy into the late hours of the night. And hotels are full as well. Parks are being used for camping, with the Kalispell tribe of about a hundred camping on the shore near the Huntington home. The Coeur d'Alene tribe has taken over one of the parks, and immediately, the sound of their singing and drumming can be heard for several blocks.

Most of those supporting Fletcher "Gunboat" O'Reilly have been arriving this morning. They are linked up with the town of Wallace and the mining operations near there. Because of the intense rivalry between the local loggers and millworkers, who generally support Blackjack Diamond, and the miners, who support Gunboat O'Reilly, there has been an increased presence of marshals and law officers throughout the area, especially at and near the high school field. No one wants to anticipate open brawling and rioting, but history cannot be ignored.

The tone of interest will be somewhat divisive in different ways: besides the intense rivalry between the lumbermen and miners, there's also the division between those who like and tolerate Indians and those who have only hatred and resentment for them. Then, there's the contrast between the religious community, which is aware of Blackjack's beliefs, and the taverns and saloons and brothels in Coeur d'Alene, where boxing and gambling are a part of their lifestyle. Though children are not generally attracted to boxing events, this occasion is different. Blackjack Diamond has become a topic among the young in the Coeur d'Alene area. The mixture of people at this fight scene will be very different than at most boxing events.

Blackjack is usually very focused before his fights. He knows why he was taunted and chased yesterday; he's always been a living battlefield in the war between evil spirits and angels. He's experienced many times the intention of evil ones trying to get him confused or distracted as he approaches the time of his fight. And he knows he must rely upon exercising faith, that his invisible friends will be near; those kindred spirits, the folks at church call angels.

Blackjack and Gunboat leave the high school where they have prepared to enter the ring. The two fighters exchange glances. They have no enmity between them, which contrasts strikingly with the factions they represent, miners and lumbermen.

As Jackson approaches the crowd that surrounds the ring, he pauses. Pop says nothing, but is curious to what is going on in his fighter's head. He knows his fighter well, but there are things he may never understand about his peculiar ways. Pop senses this is a moment Jackson is sorting something out.

As the crowd cheers the fighter's arrival, Jackson's eyes scan the crowd like an eagle scans the prairie. His head turns to his right and there stand those who pursued him into the forest yesterday. They recognize Jackson, just as he recognizes them. They talk among themselves. They're only about fifty or sixty feet from our fighter. They didn't know the one they taunted and attacked was the half-breed fighter the entire region has been waiting to see. One, probably the 'number two' who became intimate with the tree yesterday, shows some serious facial injuries. Jackson nods his approval of their presence. He has no ill feelings toward them. They made a mistake and they paid for it. He slaps his two gloves together, turns and heads to the ring. Only a slight distraction, he thinks. Time to get down to business.

As the fighters enter the ring, almost at the same moment, the loud clamor from the audience erupts. There is mutual respect shone by both of them as they meet in the center of the ring and tap their gloves together. Both of the fighters appear to be in great condition as would be expected. After introductions, the handlers and managers exit the ring. The crowd noise subsides. Everyone is waiting for the sound of the bell. RING!

As the fighters cautiously approach each other, both fighters smile and seemingly nod their approval of each other. Then they engage, exchanging a flurry of punches. Most of the boxing followers expected Blackjack to be in pursuit of his crafty opponent, as in the first fight, Gunboat keeping Jackson at bay with fast, short punches: jabs, short hooks and uppercuts. At this moment in the fight, they are wailing away at each other, both of them taking punches to the head. It would seem that neither one has kept to his fight plan, perhaps because Gunboat has decided to slug it out with Jackson, something no one expected. Usually when this happens in a fight with Blackjack Diamond, Blackjack prevails. In this first minute or so into the fight, they both seem to be giving and taking, and it's anyone's guess as to who's landing the better blows.

Then, an overhand right lands squarely on O'Reilly's cheek. His feet shift as his knees buckle and he staggers about. Jackson has the clear advantage, but seems to have something bothering his eyes. He's shaking his head and instinctively tries to rub his eyes, which is a mistake. He's making the situation worse.

Jackson plods forward, but in the few seconds he's having difficulty seeing, Gunboat recovers his senses and then goes into the strategy that was expected. He uses his footwork to evade Jackson's forward movement. Now his jabs come to meet Blackjack's advance. Round one ends and the crowd is loud and appreciative of the action they saw. In that first round, both fighters displayed their strong points, though the intense opening moments were more like a barroom brawl than a boxing match.

Rounds two through seven follow much the same pattern of their first fight two years ago. O'Reilly is outscoring Jackson, though neither fighter is landing a significant number of damaging blows. Jackson attempts to land short hooks to his opponent's body. He tries to move Gunboat's gloves and arms to the side, but in this, he fails. Gunboat's arms have taken many powerful strikes. His upper arms between his elbows and his shoulders are red and bruised, and the quickness in his feet seems to be diminishing.

"It's time to focus on those short hooks to his body," Pop tells his fighter. "Use the footwork I had you practice; it'll get you in closer to him. He's not got the quickness he had. Wear him down and take him out." Blackjack sees what Pop was talking about in his mind. He completely forgot about it. "It's time to put it all together."

Round eight starts out like the previous six, both fighters feel the help of the breather between rounds. As the seconds tick away, Gunboat gets careless. Blackjack advances his back foot, extends his front foot forward and is now within the range of landing his hooks. Three of them land in succession, and Gunboat O'Reilly finally feels the power of Blackjack Diamond. He winces and momentarily gasps for air. He backs away, knowing if he takes many more of these blows to the ribs he'll be unable to continue the fight. In desperation, he displays the veracity and aggressiveness that he did in the beginning of the fight. He's hoping for a lucky punch that will somehow cause Blackjack to weaken his attack. Blackjack has seen the effect of his body punches in every one of his fights. He knows Gunboat O'Reilly has been slowing down and that it's time to finish him off and end this fight. Too soon, the bell sounds the end of round eight.

"You hurt him. He showed it. Do that again and go upstairs and finish him off. He may have outpointed you in several of the rounds. Don't let this go to the judges. You may lose the decision, again. Get your attack going at the beginning of the round and you'll be able to finish him off. Do it. He's yours now. Don't let him off the hook. Get it done." Pop doesn't trust the judges in any fight. Crookedness and strange judging have always been in boxing, but a clear knockout solves that problem. Blackjack knows this too, and he will follow Pop's advice carefully.

As the two fighters approach each other at the beginning of round nine, Blackjack nods to Gunboat as if to say "It's been a good fight, and you've shown a lot of guts, but now it's time we end this dance." Though these words are not spoken, Gunboat gets the message and instantly tries to rely upon his ability to keep Blackjack away with his jabs and quick straight punches. For several seconds this works, as it has through most of the fight. If he could continue being effective through this round and one more, he's confident he'll get the decision. He knows that round eight might have been a turning point in the fight. And his ribs are beginning to really hurt.

It's time to reach into his bag of tricks. Jackson surprises O'Reilly with six stiff jabs in a row, two of them landing flush on his face. This surprises Gunboat and brings something new into the fight. He tries to respond with a series of jabs of his own, but Blackjack takes them well and while receiving those punches high on his forehead, he dishes out a powerful right hook to Gunboat's solar plexus. Again, Gunboat feels the power of Jackson's punch, and while making an effort to retreat, he doesn't retreat far enough. Blackjack unleashes a barrage of six punches to Gunboat's head, and he falls backwards onto his butt, before the effect of the punches actually settle in. Then he falls flat on his back. He is unconscious. His handlers quickly come to him, after throwing in the towel, signaling their fighter is through.

Blackjack Diamond has knocked out Fletcher "Gunboat" O'Reilly in the ninth round in Coeur d'Alene, Idaho. The news of Jackson's victory is sent by wire and telephone across America.

After Blackjack changes back into his clothes and is exiting the high school, he is met by nearly two hundred of his fans who want to shake his hand. They know he is about to leave the Idaho Panhandle towards Reno, Nevada, and they don't know if they'll ever see him fight again in Coeur d'Alene, as it is not known to be a main stop on the boxing circuit. Waiting in the long line for a chance to meet him are many of the natives from various tribes, who have come to support him, and of course many of the youngins from around Coeur d'Alene and the vicinity. Jackson's had Pop pick up a bag of candy to give out to the kids. Most of them won't eat the candy, but save it as a keepsake to prove that they met Blackjack Diamond.

Tomorrow Jackson will begin to focus on "Bat the Rat' Mason, his next fight. Tonight, he will celebrate his victory at the Huntington Taylor home with Taylor's family, and some of Jackson's Kalispell relatives who have made their way back to Coeur d'Alene for the fight.

It's 1 PM on Sunday and there's quite a group at the train depot to see Jackson off. And of course, Pop. Some of the Kalispell and Coeur d'Alene tribe, as well as a few from other tribes have decided to see their Indian brother depart. He has brought them the honor they had hoped for. Dozens of children are also there to see their champion fade away down the long tracks westward.

"Pop, I want to come back to Idaho," Jackson pipes up as they cross the border. He's glancing back as they've just passed Post Falls, the last town in Idaho, passing into Washington and through Spokane on their way to Portland, Oregon.

"Fifteen minutes from Coeur d'Alene and you're already moanin' about missin' Idaho. Boy, we've got business ahead of us. You have two, maybe three, fights and you'll be in line to challenge for the title. That is, iffen that big, oversize Champion will fight you." Pop has sensed that Jackson is very much at home in the Idaho Panhandle. He will keep his fighter focused on his fights from now until a title shot.

"By the way, Jackson, how did you really tear that leather shirt on Friday?" Pop knows his fighter well. He's not just his manager, he's his adopted "Pop" and he knows when his boy is not telling the whole story.

"I'll tell ya 'bout it later, Pop. It's somethin' I just don't want to talk about now, O.K?"

"I knew there was more to the story."

Beneath the Blue Damask

by Lila Bolme

Through bleary eyes she gazes off
beyond the leaded glass
and longs for all her soul still holds
beneath the blue damask

No balm of time or joyous note
behind the leaded glass
assuages sorrow's fountain lain
beneath the blue damask

The pain exquisite in its work
transcends the leaded glass
and tighter binds her soul to his
beneath the blue damask

So silver cord in trembling hand
she shuns the leaded glass
and goes to join him once again
beneath the blue damask

Saying Goodbye to a First Love

by Becca Crouse

The lake was calm. The whipping breeze had dissipated, leaving a few straggling clouds bunched in the sky like sheep without a shepherd. The sinking sun had free reign to beat down on the lake's surface, though Keith knew it would do little to warm the waters. His dry suit would help. It had damn well better; he'd needed the help of his grandson and twice the usual amount of time to put it on. It would not be a process he'd soon repeat.

His great-grandsons were waiting, splashing at each other like teenagers. Keith slowly pulled himself up from the wicker chair in the corner of the long white porch and shuffled out into the sunshine. He felt every one of the seven steps as he climbed down the stone stairs. There had been a time when he could leap to the ground, back when his limbs were sinew and green wood instead of brittle old branches. A small gust of wind brought the lake water closer and he took as deep a breath as he could. A tinge of black powder slipped in with the marine scent bringing along the memory of prior Julys.

A lifetime of Fourth-of-July celebrations unfurled across his mind like ticker tape at a parade. The first fireworks display his daughter beheld at age four, the pyrotechnic phenomenon over the Sydney Harbor on his and his wife's 50th wedding anniversary trip, watching from his naval destroyer as an Army platoon made use of M2 60mm mortars to celebrate the 4th while bogged down in Korea…all still vivid. But nothing was so firmly indented in his memories as the night he watched

Georgie Oakes drown in Coeur d'Alene Lake.

Pushing aside the memories, he focused on the short walk down to the water's edge. Today marked the last July 4th of the current millennium. After a lifetime of adventurous living, Keith never expected to make it to the year 1999. At 82-years-old and in possession of an implacable pancreatic tumor, he doubted he would last too much longer. This was fine with him. His wife, Agnes, had passed several years earlier and they'd lost their daughter, Carol, to cancer back in the 80's. They'd shared a lifetime of celebrations. He didn't find much to celebrate these days. Let the kids have their parties, he wanted one more holiday on the lake of his childhood.

Coeur d'Alene had changed in the decades since he'd left. The small town was now bustling, stuffed full with visitors from all over the world. The trendy little pubs and coffee houses spilled forth revelers of all ages and condition. It took so long for dark to fall that no one feared the night ending. Later, there'd be an edge of desperation as they tried to fit in one more thrill, something to assure themselves they'd not been shortchanged this century. That they'd lived life to the fullest. That they were still relevant.

Keith snorted. He'd moved past relevancy years before. He'd had his share of fast living, trying to hold tight to the highs and avoid the lows. It was a balm to shuffle down the winding path in the quiet part of town and remember much slower days. He had not yet been born at the turn of the last century, but the first few decades he remembered fondly.

He'd grown up in the roaring 20's. His parents insisted he attend school in the mornings, but relied on his help in the family dry goods store in the afternoons. The job was not without reward; his parents believed in adventure, in small doses, and they always included the children. One such outing had been an excursion to Harrison on the lake's most wondrous steamboat, *The Georgie Oakes*. Keith could close his eyes and see her shiny stacks, almost feel the sun-warmed rough wooden railings. *Georgie* boasted three ivory decks that seemed a child's dollhouse from far away but a wondrous miracle of architecture when pulled into dock. He'd been certain a more marvelous ship would never be built. She'd last forever.

Several years later, in 1927, it became clear that he'd been wrong. The White Star Navigation Company decided this particular sternwheeler had outlived her usefulness. *The Georgie Oakes* couldn't compete with the newer classes of steamships and so she was brought before the crowd at the annual 4th of July festival and set ablaze. The crowd gathered at Independence Point delighted in the climbing swirls of orange and red as the waves of flame consumed the first steamboat Keith had ever stood foot on.

With clenched fists, he'd watched her demise. How could such a lovely lady be discarded, humiliated, used as titillation for the masses when no longer relevant, no longer needed. She'd been outclassed by the younger ladies of the lake and no matter that she'd served faithfully for years. The inferno threatened a nearby dock and she'd been doused, left to drift into the dark, a charred and devastated shell. He'd shaken off tugging hands and stood firm until the end, a statue but for the twin trails of tears.

Years passed and Keith moved on. He joined the Navy and fell in love, both with a beautiful blonde named Agnes and a new ship. He visited Coeur d'Alene rarely. Once both his parents passed, he saw no need to return. Eventually his life slowed and he was gifted, or cursed, with abundant time for reflection.

Keith's perspective had changed as he'd reached his "sunset years." Material goods held a great deal less meaning and personal connections a great deal more. *The Georgie Oakes* had returned to him in a dream, beautiful and shining. He'd been startled to realize his view of that 1927 4th of July had transformed. Now he shuddered at the thought of such a lady being lifted from the lake, mothballed and allowed to rot as her replacements steamed over the waves. Surely her Viking funeral had been much more appropriate. She'd gone out in a blaze of glory and sunk gracefully to the bottom of the lake, a permanent fixture on the sandy lakebed.

The scent of sunbaked ponderosa pine mingled with fresh cut grass and Keith smiled. His great-grandsons hailed him from the boat dock and he made his way over. To them, this was a new adventure, a new experience to be added to their collection like beads on a string. For him, it was a chance to say goodbye to his first love. And perhaps one more bead to add to his string as well. One last bead before he'd be mothballed in a hospital bed and allowed to waste away as his body deteriorated. The sun was setting and there was no time more fitting.

The small motorboat scooted over to the dive spot. Keith's grandsons helped him into his scuba gear and put their video camera on some stick thingy so they could film the dive. There was a time when people lived their lives instead of recording them. He shook his head; why limit your view to what you could see through a four-inch window?

When everything was set, the boys fell back into the drink. He took his time and slipped into the lake like slipping into the cool sheets next to a beautiful woman. His heart beat faster. Soon he was in over his head. Below him was a dark, murky blue and to each side a cool aquamarine. He followed the fins of his grandsons. He'd spent half his life in one ocean or another and he felt like a fish in water. An old, old fish. As they dived deeper, they turned on their lights and the underwater world was revealed in small sweeps. It took time, but the boys led him to her.

Georgie waited at a depth of 42 feet. She lay on her side, her upper decks gone, and her paddle wheel only a ghost. Large pieces of her hull were missing, puzzle pieces that would never be fit back into place. Algae coated her, hiding scorch marks. A smallmouth bass darted in and back out of their light.

The boys waited patiently as Keith circled the site. He trailed shaking fingers along her side. With his eyes shut, he could again see the riverbank fly by, smell the burn of coal smoke. The slap of the paddle wheel in the water was a metronome for excited breaths and running feet. He rocked gently in the water and kept his eyes closed. His body may be failing, but his mind was as clear as ever. He pulled up memory after memory of days and nights spent exploring. This boat had shaped his life, implanted a love of the water and sailing upon it.

The ascent was slow and he turned away without a final glance. He now knew her as she was, but he chose to remember her as she'd been. He had hope others would do the same for him when his time came.

As he surfaced, Keith watched as the sun finally dropped behind the timbered hills. His grandsons treaded water next to him, ready to help him back into the boat. It was not yet time for fireworks, but he had done what he'd come to do. The Fourth had been properly commemorated. With the cancer spreading, he would not make it to the new year, so this was his Fourth of July and New Year's Eve rolled into one. He was satisfied. He'd filled this century with meaning and love and laughter and living. He and *Georgie* could rest.

Celebration in Seventeen

By Tana Essary

Blue sky
Bright sun
Silver lake
Summer fun
White house
Green lawn
After picnic
Stretch and yawn
Cool breeze
Banjo plays
Couples dance
Grandma sways
Wood canoe
Pale umbrella
Pretty girl
Rugged fella
Stolen kiss
Cheeks pink
Tippy canoe
Into the drink

Just Me, Marla

By Barbara K. Rostad

Author's Note: These are not excerpts from an actual journal; the dates are approximations, but the information contained here is primarily derived from interviews with Marla Lake. It is a factual account of her caretaking years at the Jewett House placed in a format known as creative nonfiction.

June 17, 1985

Jesus said, "In My house there are many mansions; if it were not so, I would have told you. I go to prepare a place for you (John 14:2)." But a mansion here on earth? That never crossed my mind.

Our year in Priest River led us to conclude that while lovely, it's smaller than we'd like. My husband Pete and I came to Coeur d' Alene to seek employment. Nothing was turning up. I'd heard it said that in difficult times, just open the Bible, point your finger on a verse, and help will be found there.

Well, I decided to try it. My finger landed on a verse in Matthew that basically said, "Don't worry." The message is very clear: Therefore, take no thought saying, 'What shall we eat? or What shall we drink? Or wherewithal shall we be clothed?' For your heavenly father knoweth that ye have need of all these things (Matthew 6: 31-32). A peace came over me and I stopped being so anxious about what would happen to us.

When I spotted the ad for a caretaker at a senior center with a free apartment, I thought, "Well, I've been a nurse's aide, I like seniors and I had a special relationship with my Grandma---I'm going to apply." I had no clue the job was at a 7500-square foot mansion on two acres in full view of Lake Coeur d'Alene.

Within a month we had a home with a suite of three upstairs rooms plus the downstairs kitchen and we had jobs to do. Pete got on as a firefighter. Responsibilities at the Jewett House included light housekeeping, open and close doors for scheduled activities, clean up, buy supplies, and do part of the grounds keeping.

August 28, 1988

This house has good karma. It was given to the city from such a great family. Mrs. Huntington Taylor used to make lemonade for the neighborhood kids. They could go in the basement to put on bathing suits and swim at the beach in front of the house. Both Taylors and Jewetts were generous families.

September 25, 1989

Mr. and Mrs. Duck are back. I think this is their third year. This pair comes right up on the porch. I quacked at them, opened the door and they walked right in! We got a good laugh. They hang out for a few weeks every year.

July 24, 1990.

I was out by the back porch today when a racoon came around the corner, then right behind him another emerged from around the corner and another. One at a time, single file, a whole crew of them went past me and the porch and climbed up a tree.

July 23, 1992

I've been going over the North Idaho College catalog, reviewing what all I'd need to get my RN. There's a bunch of prerequisites like English, biology, psychology, math, communication. Then the nitty gritty of the program itself like Nursing Practice I-IV. I think I'll ease my way into it with a couple of prerequisites.

October 22, 1995

I've done a lot of the required rotations now---ER, geriatrics, cancer ward. But only one nearly stopped me in my tracks toward the finish line. I have finally finished my stint at the mental hospital. Almost every night on my way home I'd say to myself, "I'm not going back." Then I'd argue with myself, saying that psychiatric nursing is important and I need to keep an open mind.

May 13, 1996

It's official! I'm an RN! No starched white caps these days but I'm eager to begin. I've been recruited from my class by Kootenai Health to be a critical care nurse. I start next week.

July 14, 1999

Friends who know I'm getting divorced have asked me if I'm scared to live in a three-story mansion by myself. These three rooms have been my home for so long now that it hasn't been very hard. I'm gone a lot to my job at the hospital plus I always have so much to do around here there's not much time to think about being scared. Besides, this bedroom is more like a retreat. There are windows on three sides. I feel like I'm in a treehouse when I'm in bed. Much as I love this house, my favorite section is my own apartment on the second floor.

August 16, 2007

I'll never tell Mom again that I'd like a collection of *anything*. Last year sometime, I mentioned I'd like to start a nutcracker collection---now I have a truckload of them! She sent my stepbrother over this week with his pickup to deliver them after she spent most of the summer yard-saling all over Montana to find them. There are tall ones—like about three feet high---and short ones---and everything in between.

Some have a foot or other part missing. Not all of them are soldiers. One is a chef, another a skier. When she comes for her annual visit, I'm going to get her picture with them.

September 22, 2007

Going nuts over nutcrackers may be kinda nutty---but boy, is Mom proud of 'em. I lined them all up on the stairs in the front hall and took her picture. What a crack-up! It's going to be fun to place them all around the house as part of the Christmas decorations.

September 14, 2009

This foot business is an ongoing struggle. Pain in my foot isn't easy to endure when I'm walking the hospital halls eight hours a day. I keep hoping it will improve, disappear on its own, because some days it's better, some days worse.

What will happen if I can't keep my nursing job? Not to mention my job here at Jewett.

July 18, 2010

The foot saga continues. My doctor thinks I have a stress fracture and wants me to stay entirely off my foot for eight weeks. For that to happen, I'd have to take a leave of absence from Kootenai. I can be off as long as six months and still return to my slot. I've been there 15 years now and love bedside nursing. Every day I tell any new patients, "My name is Marla and I get to be your nurse today."

August 17, 2010

This can't go on. Pain in my right foot just isn't going away. Should I really take a leave of absence?

September 10, 2010

Well, I finally bit the bullet. I signed up for a leave of absence and will try the eight weeks of not putting weight on my foot. Maybe then it will heal.

October 10, 2010

The old chicken coop out back is going to have a new purpose. Shared Harvest plans to use it as a greenhouse to get their veggies going early. We had a meeting about it the other day. Getting there in the wheelchair was entertaining. But I'm all for the idea. I hope it works out for them.

November 12, 2010

I will never forget putting weight on my foot for the first time after two months. Talk about excruciating! I was in the front foyer of the house. It felt like I was trying to stand on a knife. I couldn't put my foot on the carpet without a burning pain. I started to cry.

So, I went back to the doctor, who said, "That's normal, Marla."

December 8, 2010

Pushing through the pain is no picnic. My goal is to walk in circles 20 minutes at a time. I had to start out with 10 steps, then 20, then 30. I strained my ankle tendon just the same. My doctor wants me to see a rheumatologist. They specialize in the diagnosis and treatment of musculoskeletal disease and systemic autoimmune conditions.

December 16, 2010

What good friends Taffie and Lu are! They both helped get the house decorated for Christmas. Together we got all the nutcrackers displayed. I always have some on the stairs as they are visible from the entry and hallway.

January 6, 2011

RSD. Even with my nursing background, I was not familiar with that acronym but it's what the foot surgeon suspects I might have now. It stands for Reflex Sympathetic Dystrophy, a chronic pain condition in which high levels of nerve impulses are sent to an affected site. It might represent a disruption in the healing process. One of the symptoms is "burning pain", such as I've been having. It's also known as CRPS, short for another complicated acronym. But the rheumatologist thinks my burning pain could be from Reiter's Syndrome and wants me to take immunosuppressants for it. I'm passing on those. I'm not comfortable messing with my immune system.

January 8, 2011

Whoever heard of anyone with three wheelchairs? Just me, Marla. One for each level of the Jewett House where I need to work. There's no taking one from floor to floor. No elevator here. Not even a dumb waiter, which is sort of odd, given the time frame this house was built. Anyhow, I've got one wheelchair in the basement, one on the main floor and one upstairs for my apartment. The third floor I don't really have to access under these conditions.

It must be quite a sight to watch me negotiate these stairs crawling up and descending on my rear end. Fortunately, there are few witnesses to this process. I actually got pads for my kneecaps when crawling up. I put the laundry in big garbage bags and roll it down the stairs.

March 21, 2011.

First day of Spring, my favorite season. But right now, I'm too busy learning how to vacuum and to clean toilets from a wheelchair to pay much attention to whether Spring is progressing as it should.

It was great to have my Jewett House boss help me here with the housekeeping the last few months but I got the hang of it now despite the wheelchair. Fun and games.

March 28, 2011

Well, I have to face the fact that my six-month leave of absence from Kootenai Health has come to an end. No way could I go back yet. Something is still very wrong with my foot.

April 18, 2011

How grateful I am that I took out a long-term disability insurance policy. I'm still nowhere near recovered. I've signed up for vocational rehabilitation and the good news is that they'll pay for my bachelor's degree. But I always wanted to be at the bedside. How can I give that up? It's breaking my heart to think I may have to change careers.

August 25, 2011

Mayo Clinic, here I come! Their Phoenix facility is expecting me in a couple days. I'm flying down with my wheelchair and my crutches and plan to rent a car when I get there.

August 30, 2011

The people at Mayo are glad I stood my ground on no immunosuppressants. I've had another batch of tests. They have ruled out RSD.

September 10, 2011

I've started classes for my BSN at Lewis & Clark State College, Coeur d' Alene campus. Some of it I also do online. Getting this degree will expand my career options in case this foot problem prevents me from doing primary care. Right now, I'm taking just a couple courses, community health and nursing research. It's meant to be done in four semesters but I also have to focus on my physical therapy plus meet my Jewett House obligations.

September 17, 2011

What am I doing anyhow, taking classes for a B.S. in nursing when I'm still using a wheelchair and have trouble with crutches? Do I really want a desk job this degree will qualify me for? I'm a bedside nurse. If I can't do that, do I want to stay in this field?

But I have to earn a living somehow, right?

November 29, 2011.

Thank God for the McGrane Center Pool. That 92-degree water is a bigtime blessing to me now. The hospital van comes and gets me, takes me back. I'll be so glad when I can leave that wheelchair behind.

May 14, 2012

My second semester at LCSC is nearly done! Pharmacology in Nursing, Transcultural Health Care. I'm finally getting more mobile and having less pain.

April 10, 2013

Back to work at last! I've taken a position at a hospice. I've thought for a while that God wanted me to go in a new direction. During my years as a critical care nurse I often put forth efforts to support the family during crisis care. Sometimes I'd pray with them. Other times I'd hold the hand of a dying patient until they passed. I saw instances where patients should have been helped to let nature take its course. Such reflections led me to believe a hospice job would be an opportunity to maximize these skills. It's time for a change but, praise be, I can still choose working with patients. Right now, I no longer have to worry about being relegated to a desk job. It will still be a challenge, though, because I still have some courses to finish before I can receive my BSN.

May 25, 2014

Magne Cum Laude. Can you believe it? That's me, Marla. With my Bachelors at last!

November 5, 2014

Every room on the first level now has hard wood floors just as they did at the time of construction nearly a century ago. It's been a slow process. Even the kitchen did originally have hard wood floors. Layer upon layer of old linoleum lay beneath the tile that was removed. And beneath that---wonder of wonders---hard wood flooring.

March 25, 2015

The Shared Harvest people are gearing up for another growing season. They were here cleaning up the chicken coop for a new batch of herbs and vegetables. This is their fifth year using it as a greenhouse. Even though some snow lingers in the back yard, it's one more sign that my favorite season is on the way.

November 18, 2015

For the first time in nearly a century, Jewett House has sustained damages. I'm safe but I wouldn't say undamaged. I've never been so scared in my life! The wind whipped up so much noise it seemed like a jet was overhead. What a storm!

I was out calling on patients when the storm really got underway. One of them lives in a small trailer with cardboard on the windows. The whole trailer was rattling while I was with her. The radio was urging people to hunker down and stay home but I had one more patient first. It was bad enough to be out there in it, driving home after seeing patients, but when I got here, it was even worse.

I almost went up to my apartment but the storm was really raging so when I ran to the house, I went down into the basement to the Billiard Room instead. While I was down there it sounded like something fell on the garage. I stayed there 'til midnight. When I finally went upstairs, I couldn't see anything out the picture windows except branches.

A clump of three bull ponderosas were uprooted in the storm, shearing off the front porch of the house. Three inches more and the damages would have been far greater.

November 27, 2015

Jewett House is closed. There's too much storm damage to allow people to come onto the premises. I don't know how long it will take for all the repairs, but I'm not going anywhere. Lucky for me, my apartment is undamaged and so is the rest of the house. Only the porch suffered.

December 15, 2015.

It's strange not to have Christmas decorations throughout the house but what's the point? No Christmas parties here this year. I probably won't put out my nutcracker collection or the big tree with its old-fashioned ornaments. Just a few things in my own apartment—that's about it.

February 10, 2016

No Valentine parties this year. Repairs are underway though. I suggested the porch be restored to its 1917 standards. That's generally being done.

May 20, 2016

Besides my apartment, the old porch was my favorite spot in the Jewett House. And Spring is my favorite season here.

June 12, 2016

Things are more or less back to normal. I love to see the lake's blue shimmering on a sunny day. It makes me think of a favorite song, *Somewhere Over the Rainbow,* sung by a favorite artist, Iz, or, to give the mouthful version, Israel Kamakawiwoʻole. Sometimes I can't even believe I live in this town.

October 8, 2016

I think dusk is my favorite time of day by the lake. Even if the water's been choppy earlier, it usually becomes placid in the fading light. Leftover sunset colors become ever more muted as they meld into the gathering dusk. Right now, those tones blend with the turning leaves. Once we get snow, the blue dusk of winter merges with the icy blue waters.

March 10, 2017

The new activity schedule is on the website now. I suppose many historic houses have their own websites. How different from the days of the butler taking in calling cards or people phoning to find out what's going on. Or looked in the newspaper, which, unlike some other methods, is still in use. Of course, voice mail has been added to the land line here---but the phone itself remains a stationary wall model.

Chinese Mahjong is offered in a four-class series starting March 15 and happening weekly through April 5. It's a new item along with our usual staples of yoga, pinochle and tai chi for seniors. I continue to provide free blood pressure checks "Daily Upon Request". I'm also doing a "Hand & Foot" card game every Thursday, somewhat ironic in light of my past foot problems.

The Idaho Writer's League continues on the second Wednesday and the Jewett House Book Club meets the fourth Tuesday. New on a monthly basis is the Coeur d' Alene Symphony the third Friday. This is all just the weekday events. In addition, we have many weekend functions such as weddings, birthdays, anniversaries. We strive for a broad variety of activities which brings us nearly the full spectrum of seniors. What I really like best about this job is the sense of community it fosters both in myself and others.

April 19, 2017

Open heart surgery on a 95-year-old? That's what some doctor wanted to do today. It's so different from the perspective I've gained working at a hospice. People don't want to let go of life, but at hospice we are working with people wo are accepting being terminal, who want to have quality time as long as they can. We help them have the tools and education to have what they need for a quality experience. It's very rewarding. I've met some remarkable people. They are usually brave and keep their sense of humor.

May 27, 2017

People were here all day for a wedding, finally left around nine. I grabbed a muffin and spent nearly two hours talking to one of those anthology writers preparing material related to the Jewett House. She thinks I belong in the book. I told her that collection is supposed to be about the Jewett House, not my life story. But they are intertwined. Like she pointed out, my thirty-two years in this house are about a third of its existence. No one else has spent that much time here.

Not Huntington Taylor.
Not George Frederick Jewett Sr.
Just me, Marla.
For over half my life. Now is that amazing, or what?

The Second Wednesday

by Terry Robinson

down the hill from town
large house painted white
at the end of Lakeside
last place on the right

they bring pencils and pads
stories they have drafted
emotional tales of woe
the tales they have crafted

house gifted by the Jewett's
to the town they called home
for seniors to come play
let their imaginations roam

writers—their backs to the lake
listen intently to their guest
he's facing the window
distracted, doing his best

drawn to the door
by beauty of the lake
water looks too inviting
heads outside for a break

group turns toward the window
their guest has moved to the grass
all wander onto the front porch
cool beverage in their glass

writers sit under a tree
taking shelter in the shade
guest resumes his talk
realizing he's been made

each second Wednesday
work on your Hemingway

The Journey

by Larry Telles

The yearly competition among the seven sawmill companies was over. The young Deepwater Lumber Company had beaten the production of the other companies. Cheers could be heard over the five o'clock whistle and the winding down of the band-saw. Together with the unscheduled celebration, it was Friday and the end of what seemed a long work week.

Otto Kempler could hardly wait to tell Annabelle the good news. The short drive home seemed to take forever before Otto pulled up in front of the house reserved for the lumber company plant manager. He entered the back door and heard the *clunk-clunk, clunk-clunk* emanating from the new washing machine in the far corner. Droplets of water darted here and there as the agitator slapped out its monotonous tune.

Otto called out, "Annabelle!" Not hearing an answer, he called again. "Annabelle!"

"I'm in the kitchen, Otto."

A tall, competent woman stood in front of a massive stove. It squatted like a bulldog on four short legs. A crusty cast iron pot completely covered the right front burner. Occasionally fingers of flame dashed up the side of the pot as crackling and popping came from new wood in the firebox.

"I'm glad you're home," she said, without turning.

"So am I. I have great news."

Annabelle spun around to face her husband. "You won the contest!"

"Yes, we did."

In a split second Annabelle was in Otto's arms. "Now we can go to Liverpool and get my mother and father and bring them back here to Coeur d'Alene."

Otto looked deeply into his wife's sparkling eyes. "Yes, dear, your wish has come true. I will get our two steamer trunks down from the attic tomorrow."

Their quiet celebration was broken up by the tea kettle violently spewing out steam. A foot above the spout the steam became a mist and dissipated. The light gray color of the kettle was interrupted by spikes of black soot reaching upward from its nearly flat bottom. A homemade pot holder on the stove's warming shelf was in Annabelle's right hand as she moved the kettle to the rear burner.

"Wash your hands, love. Dinner will be ready in ten minutes. Then you can tell me all about your wonderful, wonderful day."

Otto stepped past the Western Electric washing machine. It undulated to the rhythm of the agitator as soapy water cascaded from its drain hose. Otto paid no mind to the billows of suds that were raising from the depths of the deep sink's slippery bottom. He knew that Annabelle was in complete control. She would wait until the stove's water-heater could recover from the nearly finished washer load before doing the dishes.

Otto took his place at the head of the table. He gave grace, then took a large helping of Annabelle's stew. Otto didn't speak until he'd taken his last bite of Annabelle's apple pie.

"I guess you would like to hear about my day?"

"Oh, yes, Otto."

"Since we produced the most lumber output for the past seven months, Deepwater won the big prize. The men at the plant will get a bonus in their paychecks, while I will get a month off. In addition, I will take a leave of another month for travel time."

"I think that is wonderful, Otto. When do you think we can go?"

"We can start packing tomorrow, my dear, and on Monday I will contact the train station to reserve tickets for a train to New York. We need to plan on getting to Pier 54 in New York City on May 1st, for the ship's return trip to Liverpool."

"What about our new house by Lake Coeur d'Alene?"

"Most of our excess lumber production will go to build the house. They will start work while we are abroad. It won't be finished until 1917. So, for the next two years we can watch the building progress every day upon our return."

Otto's conversation was interrupted by the ringing telephone in the hall.

He slid his chair back, took the cloth napkin from his lap, and put it next to his plate. By the third set of rings, he had reached the phone.

Annabelle began clearing the dishes and, as she moved around the table, tried to hear her husband's conversation. Within just a few minutes, Otto returned. "That was Mr. Weyerhimmer."

"Why was your boss calling you at the dinner hour?"

"He wanted to come by tomorrow and show us the plans for the new house by the lake."

Annabelle had the last of the dishes in her hands as she passed through the doorway into the kitchen. "Oh, how wonderful."

****

It didn't take Otto long to find the steamer trunks in the attic and bring them downstairs. He did take them all the way into the backyard to remove ten years of dust. Upon putting the key in the lock, he found that a variety of insects had made that place their home for several years. An ice pick from the kitchen cleared the keyhole of the past residents. Otto got the trunks back in the house and in the place Annabelle requested. He would leave packing up to her. Otto had accomplished all of this by twenty minutes before noon.

Walking into the hall, he picked up the telephone receiver. "I think I will call Henry while I have a chance."

The operator answered. "Number, please!"

"Yes, operator, 323 please. Thank you."

Nearly a minute passed. "Hello, Henry, Otto here. Oh, yes, I know you will be there. I'm just checking for Annabelle. Certainly, yes, I will see you on Wednesday."

Annabelle came down the stairs, "Who were you calling, Otto?"

"Henry Pendergas. He is going to take us to the train station on Wednesday, and then park our car at the mill until we get back. The trunks are ready, dear."

"Yes, I know, Otto, I heard you struggling as you were putting them in the living room."

****

The morning arrived that both of them had been waiting for. At two p.m. sharp, Henry Pendergas twisted the bronze lever on the front doorbell.

Otto let him into the front hall. "Good morning, Otto. Are you and the missus ready?"

"She is putting on her hat and should be down momentarily, Henry."

Just as the words were out of his mouth, Annabelle came down the stairs.

Henry looked at Annabelle and asked, "Shall we go?"

She looked at Otto, who nodded.

Henry left the door open. "Very well, while you two are getting into the car, I'll get your trunks. I've given us some extra time to get to the train station. Since it rained a couple of days ago, that road won't be in good shape. It isn't even decent when it hasn't rained." And Henry made for the living room.

Henry was right. The car slipped and slid down the road to the train station. Otto put one arm around Annabelle to steady her and the other hand on the edge of the door to brace himself. The touring car rocked back and forth as the wheels skated in and out of the wheel tracks made by horse-drawn carriages.

Occasionally above the engine noise, the splattering of mud on the undercarriage could be heard. "I see what you mean by the road conditions, Henry."

Henry turned his head slightly to the rear of the car. "Old Henry Ford makes a good car, but unfortunately he can do nothing about road conditions."

As Henry finished his sentence, a sound was heard that no driver wants to hear. The car lurched, nearly pulling the steering wheel from his hands. "It's our front right tire."

"Oh, dear, what happened?" Annabelle's voice quivered.

"Now, don't you worry, I'll take care of it, Mrs. Kempler."

Otto looked over the side of the car. "I think we can get out on this side, dear. There is less mud." Finding a small patch of grass, Otto stepped down, holding Annabelle by her left arm. He reached into his watch pocket, brought out his time piece, and opened it. "We have plenty of time, dear."

In the meantime Henry had the right side of the touring car jacked high enough for the bottom of the flat tire to rest clear of the mud.

"Henry, can I give you a hand somehow?"

"No, Otto, not now. I'm happy that you had a couple of small pieces of wood in the trunk. They were good to set the jack on so it wouldn't sink down into the mud."

"Are you going to take the wheel off the car?"

"No, I leave the rim on the car, which makes it much easier to replace the tire." Henry had the old tire off the rim. With a hand pump he inflated the new tire just enough to hold its shape and inserted it in the tire casing. In the process he sprinkled some powder on the inside of the casing. He then inserted the flap, making sure it wrapped around the tube and went into the casing on each side. "I wish it was a little warmer. The tire would be a little more pliable, but it's nearly inflated now."

By the time Henry had stored all of the equipment he'd used, both Otto and Annabelle were seated and ready to continue their journey.

The remainder of the ride to the train station was uneventful. Annabelle, still wrought, rested her head on Otto's shoulder while the car rocked and lunged along the gravel road.

****

As the car rounded the bend in the road, steam could be seen belching from the huge Northern Pacific Railroad engine and quickly dissipating. Workmen and passengers scurried from station to railroad car. Henry waved to a porter with a cart on wheels, and the porter helped load the two trunks onto the vehicle. The baggage car was near the end of the train, and Henry and the porter disappeared into the milling crowd.

A smiling porter helped Annabelle up the three steps and into the car. Otto and Annabelle soon found their compartment, left some personal belongings, then went directly to the dining car. They were a bit early, but sat and watched the activity on the station platform. A man with a ladder, dressed in work clothes, moved from light fixture to light fixture, lighting the kerosene lamps.

A high-pitched, shrill whistle blew. The crowd outside began to scatter. From inside the train came a distant cry, "All aboard!"

The car began to creep forward; a heavy chugging sound filled the air.

Annabelle looked out the window. "Otto, there is Mr. Pendergas walking beside the train. He's waving at us!" Otto smiled and waved back and then sat down. Henry had reached the end of the platform and soon was out of sight as the train had picked up steam.

The train whistle sounded a long blast, followed by another long one, then short, then long again. It was a Morse Code "Q." They were approaching the first railroad crossing out of the city of Coeur d'Alene. The train whistle also seemed to signal a waiter to approach their table and take their dinner order.

When Otto and Annabelle finished eating and reached their compartment, the beds had been prepared. Annabelle turned in early. Otto sat with the morning newspaper he hadn't had a chance to read. Within the hour, he too was sound asleep.

****

The first morning, Otto and Annabelle met some new friends in the parlor car after breakfast.

They met often during the trip. This couple were going to visit relatives in New York City. After dinner in the early evening on the second day, the two couples found themselves in the lounge car.

The clickety-clack, clickety-clack of the rails, together with the swaying motion, created a pleasant hypnotic trance. The lounge car was totally void of conversation. The intermittent lights seen through the car windows had long since lessened. Passengers slowly came out of their trance as the rhythm and cadence slowed. The train had stopped!

After a few minutes the conductor came through the car. "There is a large uprooted tree lying across the tracks. We have notified the next station that we need help with its removal."

Otto suggested they go to bed. "We have a big day tomorrow, Annabelle."

Annabelle woke up first. "Otto, Otto, the train is moving."

With breakfast and lunch behind them, the couple sat again in the lounge car. The conductor entered the car at one end and was heading for the door at the opposite end, calling, "Next stop, New York City."

What seemed like an eternity to Annabelle was over as the train pulled into Grand Central Station in the late afternoon on May 1, 1915.

One of the porters got Otto a new mode of transportation in New York, a Yellow Cab. A man named John D. Hertz started the company and painted his cabs yellow after he had read a study that identified yellow as being the most visible color from a long distance.

"What will they think of next?" Annabelle said.

Otto and the cab driver got both trunks safely aboard and quickly headed for Pier 54.

Two men stood at the top of the gang plank. The first appeared to be in charge. The second man held a clipboard and wrote on it as passengers passed the men.

The couple approached the men. "Hello. My name is Otto Kempler, and this is my wife, Annabelle."

"My name is Captain William Thomas Turner."

"Nice to meet you, Captain. Everything ready to sail?"

"As soon as we get our 1265 passengers and 694 crew members aboard."

Otto whistled. "That's a lot of people to keep track of." He took Annabelle by the arm. "Thank you, Captain. Let's go, dear."

"Thank you for sailing with us, Mr. and Mrs. Kempler. Welcome aboard the R.M.S. *Lusitania*. [1]

---

* The RMS Lusitania set sail for Liverpool on Saturday, May 1, 1915. The Lusitania was sunk by

German U-boat U-20 on Saturday, May 7, 1915. It was torpedoed 120 miles off the southern coast of Ireland and went down in 18 minutes. There were only 761 survivors. Germany had waged war against the U.K., who had implemented a naval blockade of Germany. Before the ship sailed, the German embassy placed warnings in American newspapers that the Lusitania would be a target if it was carrying war munitions. It was reported that the ship contained nearly fifty tons of munitions when it sailed. The original captain, Daniel Dow, suffering from stress (tired and ill) was replaced by a new commander for the voyage, Captain William Thomas Turner. The two fictional characters in my story arrived safety in Liverpool.

If Timber Could Talk

by Jesse Warburton

This centennial abode
built of the wood of many trees
scattered across this northern region,
each tree from a different place
with a different story,
of what it might have witnessed
of the pristine beauty of this northern paradise.

With invisible eyes you saw
high in mountains that rise in every direction,
snow and ice melting,
seeping down into meadows,
flowing into streams that gush forth,
Winding through hills and into the valleys,
finding their way to the rivers and lakes,
repeating again and again,
the rhythms of endless, changing seasons.

With invisible eyes,
you viewed the villages of the earliest human inhabitants,
smoke rising from the fires of their camps
along the lakeshore and riverbanks,
their canoes and long boats on a fishing venture,
harvesting for the needs of the coming winter.

With invisible ears
you heard the sound of their voices, at times uniting,
rising in the singing of their celebrations
with the rhythm of their heartbeats pounding on their drum. Occasional intruder of different dress, different skin, different thoughts
making camp briefly, then gone.
If you could speak of what you might have seen as you stood tall, you
might tell of the flight of the birds of prey; the eagle, hawk, osprey
you heard the early morning chirping, of others flying to and fro,
busy at the dawn of their day
and the raven, his squawking call to his companions
and the softer coo of the dove
when in the night, the hoot of the owl warned, not all are sleeping
hearing at times
from out of a peaceful calm,

the whispering of the wind,
passing through the branches of every tall elder around you,
making sweet music
with the breeze that passes through their boughs
soft now, but not always so.
At times you heard the sound of the raging wind,
silencing the voices of the creatures below,
life scurrying about to their hiding places,
escaping the fierceness of a storm that damages and destroys
then finally into the brief calm of a new silence,
before life reappears
waiting for nature to unveil her next offering.

Then there were the voices of men
and the sound of the saw that severed you from your roots
to lay you down to be sawed again into lumber;
planks, boards and blocks
to become the walls, roof, ceilings, porches, and furniture
becoming this home
all that is wood from the timber of those trees
that stood like gods watching,
swaying in the wind,
witnessing change.

of all of those many trees,
you were assembled into this abode,
outwardly witnessing the changes brought by human progress,
the tempo of life speeding up to accommodate growth,
from villages into towns and cities,
paths into roads and rails,
waterways becoming busy with harvesting and shipping
and inside these walls
did you hear sweet music and singing,
laughter and applause,
the shouting of angry words
and the whispering of secrets
the sobbing of a broken heart
and the moaning of a mother giving birth, then the first crying of her newborn
the last words of a dear one dying, and the mournful weeping after
from each generation, passing on to another
witnessing the vital spirit of the human experience,
those invisible eyes peering outward to the lake and beyond
and the story of the life that has been within these walls…
oh, but only if timber could talk.

Below Red Elevation

by E.G. Moore

Fletchra glared at the "Do Not Descend" signs floating near her. They made a grid pattern that spanned for miles. The bulb on her dash flashed a warning. Her pointer finger tap, tap, tapped on her Libertycraft steering bar. She inhaled and exhaled, her breath coating the thin mask surrounding her face.

The pale cast of her mom's face crowded Fletchra's mind. She swallowed away the tears threatening to emerge, and instead hardened her thoughts to her father. She'd do anything to locate him, to get him or his benefit card back to Spokane Center and approve the cost of health care her mom needed to live. He'd bothered to set up auto payments for the hover station docking fee of *Old Ebba*, their three-hundred-year-old family aircraft created from the bowels of a 1916 steamboat. He hadn't bothered to provide any necessities for his wife and daughter. Fletchra ground her teeth.

He wasn't supposed to be gone this long. Fletchra shook her head to wash away the mental justification. What kind of man provides for his machines, but not for his family? He knew the risks when he took the science mission. His soft good-bye and long hug clung to Fletchra like a second skin, as though it'd been but a moment ago, not three years. She huffed. The mask fogged again.

"Look for the house," her mom had whispered the night before. "It's on the North shore of the lake. Lakeshore. White..." She'd swallowed hard, her chest rattling. Then her eyes clouded. "He'll be there. A wide front porch. A... An... old house there by the lake." She'd closed her eyes then, a smile simmering on her face as she drifted toward sleep. Fletchra had gripped her favorite mini pipe wrench nestled in her trouser pocket. Her dad had always teased her that she needed to make her own luck, and it was superstitious to think an inanimate object could offer her any.

Her hand mimicked that flexing grip on the steering bar now. She gazed out at the vast orange haze festering over what was once a bustling city. Her elementary education missives reverberated in her ears. She was about to fly into poisonous air. Trees so genetically altered by pollution that they'd turned into toxin factories. They covered the remains of the Inland Northwest. That's why the humans that had survived lived in the air, moving from station to high territory and back again. She missed the days when her father was the captain and she was the lead mechanic, kicking and shoveling and fixing *Old Ebba* all the way to the Montania territory. They'd port over cloth and medicine for fresh produce and coal sticks. Maybe when her father returned, they'd do it again.

But first she had to find him.

She smoothed out the wrinkled brown map she'd snatched from the Spokane Center museum, along with the breathing machine and several bags of water pods and freeze dried food. They'd never miss a few extra rations. She leaned over it, shifting her face to avoid the glare from the sun on the mask lens. If her calculations were correct, she should be close to the northern end of Lake deCoeur.

"STOP!" boomed a robotic voice. Fletchra's attention snapped up from the map. Elevation control, four bots, floated alongside the signs, punchers pointed at her. She'd been warned of this, and been told they wouldn't follow her below the hazard line. The old station master better have been right. One hit in the steam pipe, and the Libertycraft would lose steering and be retrieved.

She fluttered her finger on the steering bar, subtly moving the Libertycraft down. When she paralleled the bots, she flashed her lamplight at them, signaling surrender. They lowered their weapons and moved in to grab her machine. She watched them glide closer, biding her time. Two yards. One. The closest bot reached out a metal claw.

Fletchra jerked the steering bar forward and down. The Libertycraft responded like lightening, plummeting into the unknown. She grinned at the rush of her modifications. The flood of air on the engine box acted as a boost. Gravity unexpectedly grabbed a hold of Fletchra, yanking at her arms, head, and breath. She lost her balance at the Captainstance, and her body rammed into the steering bar. A snap echoed in the cabin, and Fletchra gasped. Rushing gray beat against the windshield. Fletchra willed herself up from the floor, the new bruise at her side throbbing. Something brushed the Libertycraft, jostling her to the right. She grabbed the dash to steady herself. She searched the floor, the space where the steering bar should have been, and growled in dismay when the bar slid aimlessly at her feet. If the Libertycraft crashed and toxins got inside before she could get in the hazmat suit, she'd be as endangered as the city.

A grating sound beat the bottom of the hovercraft, snapping her into action. Fletchra dove behind the Captainstance, yanking the handle of the closet. The hazmat suit crinkled as she ripped it from its rusty hook and flung it over her shoulders. The Libertycraft slammed into something, glass crackling. It twisted her feet from under her. Stars burst across her vision. She snapped her eyelids shut, and willed the journey to end. Glass shattered. She forced her aching arms into the suit. The buttons fumbled in her fingers. A blow on the craft's tail sent her spinning. She threw her arms around her neck. The buttons materialized there, and she snapped them into the matching halves of the breathing machine that wrapped her head. A loud suck and blub meant the tubes had connected and synchronized. A rush of oxygen flooded her senses.

The Libertycraft smashed to a stop in its final resting place. Fletchra imagined poison leaking into her skin. She needed her gloves. Feeling down her body, she found them still chained to her trouser belt loop. Instinctively, she reached into a pocket and sighed at the comfort of her lucky wrench. The skin of her hands burned and itched from the toxic air. She forced her fingers into the gloves and snapped the suits sleeves in place round them.

She lay back, grinning at the cracked windshield. The bulb on her dash flashed to let her know she'd made it. Her breathing slowed, clouding the thin mask skewed on her face. She'd done it. She'd gotten below the red elevation level and didn't even accidently land in the lake.

Now to retrieve her dad.

One rough movement at a time, Fletchra moved to standing again. She corrected the mask, search and retrieved the map, and tried to push the hatch outward without success. Something had it wedged tight. To the windshield then. She pulled out her lucky wrench and swung it like a baton at the remaining glass to clear the way before depositing it in her pocket again. Jumping out, she landed on squishy ground. Chirps permeated the air, and bugs burst from the gray fog around her. They pummeled her suit and mask. She squealed and swatted at them, moving a few steps from the Libertycraft in hopes of getting away from them. Eventually, the thumps on her body subsided to a few small ones on her lower legs, followed closely by a breeze. Where was the Libertycraft? She should have kept a cool head and checked it over before she moved away from it. How off earth would she get home if she didn't find anything down here?

She sighed, and pulled the map closer to her face. She needed to find a street sign or some other important landmark. A lot of the roads near the lake house, notated on the map as "Jewett," had numbered names. She still walked on ground, but the hard surface of a road must be nearby. She wandered through the fog, keeping a keen eye out for structures or obstacles. The breeze should have cleared the fog, but it only seemed to swirl it and obscure the view worse.

Why was the ground so wet? Fletchra wondered. The ground near the lake was hilly, with the water hardly ever reaching this high in the cold seasons. At least that is the impression her father's tales portrayed. She reached into her pocket to grasp her mini wrench, and plunged ahead. Her boot caught in pooled water and concrete, slamming her head into a pole. She fell backward into the water, and thanked God her suit consisted of a water-resistant layer. She scrambled to her feet, and glanced at the sign attached to her vertical nemesis. 11th Street and Lakeshore. Fletchra grinned and glanced again at her map. She ran her finger over crease and fold, landing on her location. From there, she followed Lakeshore to "Jewett." Nodding, she looked up at her surroundings, and stepped in the direction of her destination. If her mom was sure that her dad was there, then he must be. Fletchra splashed through the shin-high water, content with the hard, if slimy, surface underneath it. She waded on and on, catching sight of pointed fence posts and swampy trees between currents of fog.

A large splash to her left forced a pause. Fletchra cast her gaze around her, noticing ripples from the direction of the noise beating her boot.

"He-llo?" she breathed out the words like a question, and almost kicked herself for how pathetic she sounded within the mask. She strained to hear anything else, and satisfied, continued to wade through the water. The wind increased, churning the water's surface and giving a bit more sight ahead of her. Fletchra whooped with joy when she came to an open gate with a simple plaque swinging from it stating "Jewett." Beyond it, light flickered. Why hadn't she noticed it before? She watched it a moment, hesitating at the gate. It wasn't Morse code or air sailor signing. She racked her brain for any other pattern that might confirm that a human ran it. She quickened her soggy steps and curved along the path toward the structure.

Her mother had described it perfectly. A wide porch and peeling white paint made Fletchra proud to have found it. The light shone from within a thick layer of plastic along one window. Shadows danced in the room, jerky and awkward. It must be the plastic, warping survivors' movements. She quickened her pace, took the wide steps two at a time and landed on a slippery slab of cement in front of a shattered glass door. She rushed to the secondary door and attempted to open the knob.

A hand slapped the window just above her own. Fletchra screamed and jumped back, her chest pounding. The hand's skin was milky white and warted, with long nails ragged with use. She peered into the glass to see what was attached to the hand, for the first time thinking about the possibility that the toxins that had sent the population into the air had altered any survivors.

A face emerged in the dark of the foyer. Matted hair and torn clothes framed a thin, drawn face. Fletchra smiled. Master Piller, her dad's occasional first mate! He grinned at her, a lopsided thing so unlike him that her stomach knotted. Beyond him, slivers of light shone from under the door that must lead to the room where the light had flickered from.

"Fletchra? Fletchra!" Her Dad's voice wafted out to her. "Don't open the door!" She glanced about, eager to see her father. Where was it coming from? Why not open the door? She refocused on Master Piller, who now grasped and swiped at the door knob like he'd not seen one before. The dark of his eyes collided with hers. Lifeless eyes, predatory eyes. She moved away slowly, glancing behind only enough to not tumble down the stairs.

Large hands snagged her shoulders. Fletchra screamed, swirling to beat the threat and escape. She writhed away from the gloved hands.

She paused at her name. Her dad stood before her, trousers rolled to his knees, no hazmat suit, like a ghost among the tendrils of vapor. His benefit card dangled from a lanyard around his neck.

"How is this possible?" Fletchra whispered. Had the toxins somehow whisked her brain through the suit? Had she knocked something loose on her descent?

"I'll explain more soon, but right now all I need to know is where is your craft?" His rushed words beat her awe like a wrench knock on a steam box, violent but effective.

"It's down the road, but I crash landed." Fear gripped her, followed by relief. If he needed a vehicle, then he'd not come back because he couldn't. Even as he turned and walked down the porch steps, Fletchra followed. She tackled him with a big hug, nearly knocking them both into the sludge at their feet.

"Dad, I've missed you," she said, all anger dissolving into the toxin puddles at her feet.

"I've missed you too, Master Mechanic." His half grin still crinkled the skin by his eyes. Fletchra pulled back. "Now, let's go get my tools and get out of here."

He rushed around the house, fighting bushes and tree limbs. Another light shone back here, low and yellow, from an outbuilding. Her dad moved several large items and pressed open a door just enough to lean in and retrieve a standard issue canvas tool kit. Fletchra silently cursed herself for not bringing her own on this little trip.

Fletchra lead the way through the sledge down Lakeview Drive in silence.

"The toxins effected everyone but me," her dad said. "Master Piller, Stewart, everyone became dumb and animalistic. And they aren't even as bad as the mindless that missed the first airboats. I'm still trying to figure out where they came from, since by now those that lived at that time must have died. We came down here looking for a cure to the problem so civilization could return to the ground, and we had it the whole time in my genes." He chuckled, shaking his head.

When they arrived to the Libertycraft, her dad whistled. "That's some crash, Master Mechanic. Not sure if the windshield will make a difference, but we'll patch up the steam pipes and steering bar. Here." He handed her two metal patches and a personal torch. It was like fixing Old Ebba with him again. As she took them from his hands, she said, "We have to get this fixed and get to Mom. She's sick."

It was her dad's turn to pause. "How sick?"

"Very. You didn't leave us any access…"

He cut her off. "I know. I didn't expect to be gone that long." He swung a punch at the Libertycraft and cursed when he contacted with a thud. "Well, let's get this thing running!" he blurted.

Despite the cold sludge surrounding her feet, Fletchra found herself sweating as she sheered the Libertycraft back together. Her dad coaxed a fire from the last bundle of coal sticks, heating up the water tank and making their machine puff to life.

A thrash of water sounded from the depths of Lake DeCoeur, bigger than her earlier encounter. Her dad snapped his attention in that direction and spat out, "Fletchra, get in the craft now!"

She scrambled to obey, slipping into the Captainstance and taking the steering bar. Gauges fluctuated, and the bulb on the dash flickered to life.

Her dad shouted, and something collided with the Libertycraft, jerking it to the side. Fletchra caught herself before tumbling over, and screamed, "Dad!"

"Fly Fletchra! Get this thing off the ground!"

"I'm not going without you! Mom needs you! I need you!" She replied, grasping the steering bar with both gloved hands.

"Now!" he screeched, cut off from answering further by some unseen battle.

Fletchra willed the steam to billow, to fill the pipes. "Yes!" she hissed as the gauges lit up and the Libertycraft pulled from the muck with a sucking sound. "Get in!" she screamed, one hand on the steering bar and the other clinging to the lucky wrench in her pocket.

Her father flew through the hole where the windshield used to be and landed on the floor beside her. Another figure wiggled in halfway, thrashing milk white hands about the cabin and roaring. Fletchra pulled out her wrench, bashed it several times onto the creature's head, and pushed it out the way it had entered. The Libertycraft jerked skyward, and she glanced back to see her dad manning the steering bar, upright and commanding.

"Now, let's get to your mom!" he stated.

Fletchra sat down and nodded. She'd done it, and they'd be there within the hour to get Mom the help she needed. Maybe her mini wrench held some luck after all.

Jewett House Nickel Tour

by Terry Robinson

"Brad, what are you doing?"

"Just drying off." With the August sun setting, the North Idaho evening air carried a slight chill. After a day of swimming at Sanders Beach, Brad didn't want to say goodbye to Beth. He knew her a bit from school, but this was the first day they had spent a significant amount of time together.

"Come over to the fire. It's warm!"

Her smile was welcoming and he wondered where the night might take them.

"Hey, are you warmed up?"

Brad sat on the sand next to her, leaning against an old log. She leaned against him and rested her head on his shoulder. It felt good to be with her, and he wished the evening wouldn't end.

"I'm tired, Brad. The sun was hot today."

"I know. I'm wiped out, too." Her bare legs were stretched out in front of her and he lusted to touch their sculpted curves. She had been out in the sun most of the summer and had achieved a perfect deep-bronze tan.

"Did you hear that Potlach just gave the Jewett House to the city?" she said.

"Why would they do that? It's got to be worth a fortune."

"I know. My dad says they wanted to provide a place where the old people can hang out and play cards. I think it's pretty cool. I'd love to get married there someday!"

"I guess. Looks like nobody's home. Do you want to check it out?" He knew they were not supposed to trespass on the property adjoining Sanders beach, but with Beth's keen interest, he thought it might be exciting.

Her green eyes lit up. "Sure!" She got up, took his hand, and pulled him up.

As they walked up the beach toward the house, Brad could feel the warmth of her hand. She held his hand firmly, but not too tight. He wasn't planning to let her go anytime soon.

"Look at those big windows, Brad. Wouldn't you love to look out those all day, watching the lake?"

As Brad stepped onto the sidewalk, Beth tripped on the curb and fell against him. Standing there holding her, he instinctively bent down and kissed her. He had kissed many girls and could tell by the way Beth pushed up against him and kept the kiss going longer, that she liked him.

When they were finished, she stepped back, still holding his hand, and said, "That was nice."

"Yeah. Me, too."

She led him over to the center of the lawn and sat down. Brad sat next to her and could feel his body changing. The muffled voices of their friends, still sitting by the fire, drifted across the lawn and reached them more as tones than words. It was dark outside, but he could see her clearly in the moonlight. Beth put a hand on each of Brad's shoulders and pushed him back onto the lawn and then lay on top of him. He could feel her heart beating as she placed her moist lips against his. Her long, soft auburn hair was lying on his cheek. Brad's mind raced with thoughts of where the night was headed. He slipped his hand under her tee shirt and began slowly working his way up.

"Who's there?" A man's voice bellowed out as the front porch lights came on. "What are you two doing down there? This is private property!"

Brad pulled his hand out from under Beth's shirt and jumped to his feet. "We're just sitting on the grass. Sorry, we didn't think anyone lived here." The voice came from a man who seemed about the age of Brad's grandfather, which would have made him around eighty years old. He had a scraggly beard and a mop of unruly white hair.

"I live here. I'm the caretaker. Are you really here for the lawn, or are you smitten with the house? Many are, you know. Nothing wrong with that. This house has lots of stories."

"Well, Beth wanted to get a better look at the house, since we heard the city owns it now."

"What's your name, boy?"

"Brad, sir."

"Well, Brad, why don't you and your girlfriend come up here on the porch and I'll tell you about the house."

"Sir, she's not really …" Beth had gotten up from the grass and had hold of Brad's hand. Before he could finish the sentence and clarify that they were just friends, she gave him a steely stare while squeezing his hand. She led him up the steps to the porch and they sat on an old wood-slat swing hung from the ceiling rafters.

"Tell me about the house, sir. I love this house." She had a charming manner, and the old guy seemed to take a shine to her.

"Young lady, you've picked a good house to fall in love with. This house has a history. It was built in 1917 at a time when the big industry here in Coeur d'Alene was timber. The Rutledge Mill was located just down the beach a bit, where the golf course is now. The timber-baron plant owner built this house for his plant manager—Mr. Huntington Taylor."

Beth was fully engaged with the caretaker's story and asked, "Then why isn't it called the Taylor house?"

"That's a good question. The mill wasn't all that profitable, and after a few years the owner brought in a new Harvard-educated manger from back east—his grandson, I believe. Anyway, his last name was Jewett and the house has been known as the Jewett house ever since. Come around 1930 they closed the local mill, and all the operations were moved down to Lewiston. At some point, Mr. Jewett was moved down there as president of the whole company. From about that time on, the house was mostly used by company executives for vacations and staff retreats, but no one has really lived in it since then."

"That's sad," said Beth, "having the house empty like that."

"I'm old enough to remember the steamships on the lake, too. They would pass right in front of this house, taking logs to the mill. Off in the distance you could see ferry steamers taking passengers and cargo down the lake to the St. Joe River, where many wealthy people from Spokane would vacation. They'd arrive in downtown Coeur d'Alene by train and then catch the ferry where the big resort hotel is now. Eventually roads were built to the small towns around the lake and people began traveling by car. That was sort of the end of the steamer era. They lie at the bottom of the lake now."

"Then in the sixties we had the unlimited hydroplane races right out in front of Tubbs Hill over yonder. Oh, boy, were those boats loud! And fast! They ran those Diamond Cup Regatta races from 1958 until 1968. I hope they come back again sometime. Having a hundred thousand visitors in town makes for an exciting weekend!"

Beth had moved over to the parlor picture window and was looking through it into a darkened room. "Do you think you could turn the lights on so we can see what it looks like inside?"

"I can do better than that, young lady. I'll give you the nickel tour. Follow me."

They followed him to the front door, where he fumbled clumsily with a handful of keys on a large silver keyring. After a few seconds he pushed the front door open and turned on the lights. It was as if the house came to life. With its high ceilings, ornate crown molding, polished wood floors and grand fireplace mantels—this was a home built for someone important.

"If you'll follow me, please; we're currently in the front foyer. The parlor is to the left, with the sun room beyond. The dining room is to the right and then the kitchen is through the butler's pantry in the dining room toward the back of the house." He stood there for a second, letting us take in the expansiveness and beauty of the house. "So what do you think?"

Beth took Brad's hand and led him into the parlor. "What do I think? Can't you just hear the music? Dance with me, Brad!" She put her arms around his waist and began moving to the beat of the imagined music. He played along and with his hands on her shoulders, moving to the rhythm of her body.

"It's such an old house," Beth said, "but I can definitely see myself living here. And sitting here looking out these windows at the lake all day. Wouldn't that be great, Brad?"

"It's a cool house."

She had stopped dancing and wandered into the hallway. "What's upstairs?" she asked.

"Upstairs? Let me see, there's six bedrooms and three baths. Then on the third floor, there are servant quarters, which now is the apartment I stay in. I can't really take you up there though."

Beth was smiling. "You're lucky to live in this house."

"I'm just happy they've kept me on. Okay, you kids, it's getting late and I'm an old man. Time to say goodnight."

Beth said, "Thanks for the tour and the history lesson. This is a special place."

"It's been my pleasure, young lady. You kids enjoy the rest of your evening. And don't go sitting on any private lawns!"

As they walked across the lawn, Brad turned and waved to the caretaker. His mind turned back to Beth and the pleasure they had enjoyed earlier on the lawn. He was trying to think of a way to get things started up again.

She turned to him and said, "It's getting late. My parents will be expecting me. Can you drive me home now?"

"Sure. Do you want to do something tomorrow?"

"Yeah, but we'll have a hard time matching the Jewett House nickel tour!"

The 1916 – 1917 Small Town Outlook

by Larry Telles

Standing on the vast porch, sounds of small rippling waves couldn't be heard from the lake. The still water in summer was calm except for the occasional tug boats pulling barges filled with downed trees. The chugging of their engines passed over the lake surface toward the old grand house. Its cargo, lumber heading for the mill and then parts unknown. This sleepy little town produced wood for the expansion of a building boom across the United States. More than a decade after the turn of the 20th Century, cities and towns beyond Coeur d'Alene were expanding. Not much happening here, but the rest of the world progressed. The U.S. was not yet at war, but it was only a matter of time. The railroads were the lifeline of the country. Henry Ford made a slight difference. The automobile was wonderful, but the non-existent roads were not. Airline service wouldn't be available until 1925.

So small town America, sooner or later, heard what the world was doing beyond its city limits.

1916
January 1	2nd Rose Bowl: Washington State beats Brown 14-0.
January 5	Austria-Hungary offensive against Montenegro.
January 7	German troops conquer Fort Vaux at Verdun.
January 10	In retaliation for President Woodrow Wilson's recognition of the Carranza government, members of Pacho Villa's revolutionary army take 17 American mining engineers from a train and shoot 16 of them in cold blood.
January 17	Rodman Wanamaker organizes a lunch to discuss forming a golfer's association (later the PGA) at the Taplow Club, Martinique Hotel, New York City.
January 29	1st bombing of Paris by German Zeppelins takes place.
February 5	Enrico Caruso recorded "O Solo Mio" for the Victor Talking Machine Company.
February 8	Baseball's National League votes down Charlie Ebbet's proposal to limit 25 cent seats at the ball park.
March 15	General Pershing and 15,000 troops chase Villa into Mexico, and stay for 10 months.
March 25	Jess Willard fights Frank Moran to no decision in 10 for heavyweight boxing title in NYC.
March 25	Women are allowed to attend a boxing match.
April 1	1st US national woman's swimming championships held.
April 8	Norway approves active and passive female suffrage.
April 10	The Professional Golfers Association of America (PGA) is founded in New York City.
April 24	Ernest Shackleton and five men of the Imperial Trans-Antarctic Expedition launch a lifeboat from uninhabited Elephant Island in

	the Southern Ocean to organize rescue for ice-trapped ship Endurance.
April 30	Germany ratifies bill bringing in Daylight Saving Time - first country in the world.
May 5	U.S. marines invade Dominican Republic, stay until 1924.
May 20	Codell, Kansas hit by tornado (also on same date in 1917 & 1918).
May 20	Saturday Evening Post cover features Norman Rockwell painting.
May 21	Britain begins "Summer Time" (daylight saving time).
May 27	President Woodrow Wilson addresses the League to Enforce Peace, founded in 1915, and gives public support to the idea of a league of nations.
June 6	Voters in East Cleveland approve women suffrage.
June 15	Boys Scouts of America forms.
June 24	Mary Pickford becomes first female film star to get a million dollar contract.
June 26	Cleveland Indians experiment with numbers on their jerseys (one game).
June 29	Boeing aircraft flies for 1st time.
July 1	Coca-Cola brings current coke formula to the market.
July 15	Boeing Company (Pacific Aero) formed by William Boeing in Seattle, Washington.
August 25	U.S. Department of Interior forms the National Park Service.
August 29	Congress creates US Naval Reserve.
September 1	U.S. Keating-Owen Act (child labor banned from interstate commerce).
September 3	U.S. President Woodrow Wilson signs Adamson Act, providing an 8-hour day on interstate railroads, preventing a national railroad strike.
September 6	1st true supermarket, the "Piggly Wiggly" is opened by Clarence Saunders in Memphis, Tennessee.
September 7	Workman's Compensation Act passed by Congress.
September 17	The Red Baron [Manfred von Richthofen], WWI flying ace of the German Luftstreitkräfte, wins his first aerial combat near Cambrai, France.
October 2	San Diego Zoo founded.
November 7	Jeannette Rankin (Rep-R-Mont) elected to Congress as its first woman Representative.
November 19	Samuel Goodwyn and Edgar Selwyn establish Goldwyn Pictures (the company later became one of the most successful independent filmmakers).

1917

January 28	Municipally owned streetcars take to the streets of San Francisco, California.
February 15	San Francisco Public Library (Main Branch at Civic center) dedicated.

February 26	1st jazz records recorded - "Dixie Jazz Band One Step" and "Livery Stable Blues" by Original Dixieland Jazz Band for the Victor Talking Machine Company.
March 19	United States Supreme Court upheld 8-hour work day for railroad employees.
March 31	United States purchases Danish West Indies for $25M & renames them Virgin Islands.
April 4	United States Senate agrees (82-6) to participate in WWI.
April 6	United States declares war on Germany, enters World War I.
May 4	A flotilla of U.S. destroyer ships arrive in Queenstown, Ireland, to aid in convoying ships to England.
May 10	Atlantic ships get destroyer escorts to stop German attacks.
May 18	United States Congress passes Selective Service Act, authorizing the federal government to raise a national army for the American entry into World War I through compulsory enlistment.
May 30	Jazz standard "Dark Town Strutters Ball" by Original Dixieland Jazz Band first recorded.
June 5	Million U.S. men begin registering for draft in WWI.
June 8	Walt Disney graduates from Benton High School.
June 12	Secret Service extends protection of president to his family.
June 26	1st U.S. Expeditionary Force arrives in France during World War I.
July 20	WWI draft lottery held; #258 is 1st drawn.
August 5	The entire US National Guard is taken into national service, subject to presidential rather than state control.
August 14	China declares war on Germany and Austria.
September 3	1st night bombing of London by German aircraft.
October 15	Dutch dancer Mata Hari is executed by firing squad for spying for Germany during WWI at Vincennes near Paris.
October 17	1st British bombing of Germany.
October 19	Love Field in Dallas, Texas is opened.
October 27	20,000 women march in a suffrage parade in New York, U.S.
November 1	In WWI, the 1st U.S. soldiers are killed in combat.
November 3	1st class U.S. mail now costs 3 cents per ounce.
November 6	New York State adopts a constitutional amendment giving women the right to vote in state elections.
December 1	Boys Town founded by Father Edward Flanagan west of Omaha Nebraska.
December 18	The 18th Amendment, authorizing prohibition of alcohol, is approved by the US congress and sent to the states for ratification.
December 19	1st NHL game played on artificial ice (Toronto).
December 26	U.S. Federal government took over operation of American railroads for duration of WWI.

News Worth Living For

by E.G. Moore

Sarah sipped from the elaborate tea cup with equal parts delicacy and efficiency. If she managed to drop it, she and Alfred would have no way to pay for it, but heaven forbid the other women present notice her death grip on the handle. She frowned at the cup, and subtly loosed the fancy leaves caught up in her teeth with her tongue. Another step toward the fireplace, the second time around the room. She took her time to avoid getting light-headed, casually milling among Coeur d'Alene's elite females with only one goal: listen in case Alfred called for her.

He'd been acting strangely since the law firm he'd apprenticed with closed. She'd hoped the trip out to Idaho to see his classmate would ease him, but his brother's curt, antagonizing letters seemed to unnerve him further. The study he hid in held just enough furniture and just enough ambiance of a cave to offer him reclusive comfort.

"Hello Sarah," a postured woman in a wide-brimmed hat said, easing a hair too close. Sarah forced a smile.

****

Alfred leaned against the study's roughhewn mantel, a brandy-filled glass in one hand, and a crisp white paper in the other. His sips hardly helped the ache in his chest, but the burn eased some of his guilt. The heavy door beside him muffled the clatter of tea cups on saucers and high-pitched chatter from the receiving room. Thank God, his schoolmate's lake house was grand enough he could hide in here. Anything to avoid the stilted conversation of women cooped up like hens from the blustery fall weather.

He set the letter on a cluttered work desk, careful to avoid John's half-smoked cigar crumbling in a glass ash tray. Alfred couldn't stand the scathing words of his brother any longer. Blue squiggles crowded his vision as it had been more and more often, almost burning this time.

The doctors had encouraged him to calm down when the headaches threatened. He breathed deeply in and out of his nose, trying to ignore the branches scraping along the windows of the office, and then took a large gulp from his glass. Perhaps this drink would wash away the news that he'd never be a father and his sweet wife Sarah would never be a mother. And the next one would drown his brother's insistence that he come back east and rejoin the assembly line. Him, a laborer again, after all the schooling he still needed to pay off. He'd always been sure he'd been made for more, and the lawyer internship had been promising. Until the firm closed.

He tipped the glass again. Nope, that last swallow hadn't splashed away the ping of frustration like he hoped either. Blue lines again, stronger and brighter this time, clouding over the fireplace, and making his imagination stir in the flames. What he wouldn't give to be free of it all.

A footstep-like creak behind him made him jerk. The scatter of glass over his wool stockings startled him almost as much. Blast! He'd not meant to drop it. He mustn't let the weather and sour mood get to him like that.

****

The shatter of glass in the next room rang out over the guests, silencing them. Sarah made eye contact with a few of the ladies, set down her cup on the closest surface, and stepped to the door. She hesitated, her hand posed over the brass knob. With a sigh, she pressed open the door and peeked in on Alfred.

"Are you alright?" she asked, a forced hush hovering behind her.

Eyes bright and hair disheveled, Alfred looked every bit a lunatic. "Yes, yes," he muttered. She softened to him, noticing the stain on his shirt and the sparkle of glass at his feet.

"Are you sure?" she frowned at him, casting her eyes to each of his, then to the set of his jaw, and then to his heaving chest.

She glanced about the room, looking for anything out of place or that could be used as a weapon. Doctor Jeffrey had warned that should his headaches and accidents continue, she needed to be aware of opportunities for physical self-affliction.

Alfred gestured for her to return to her socializing, attempting to sooth her with a half-spirited grin. Ever the obedient wife, she sighed again and gently closed the door. He'd never try something with so many witnesses in the next room, she reassured herself.

****

Sarah had slipped back out of the room soft as a house mouse, and he was grateful for it. Alfred pressed the door closed behind her with palms and forehead. Could he spoil anything else for them?

"Yessss," a hiss answered, and a series of creaks along the floor echoed the earlier one. This time, he slowly turned, hoping to catch the speaker off guard. A flash of blue alighted the room, and he shook his head to clear his vision.

The study was empty but for the shattered glass, shining from the recently polished floors. He moved toward the bathroom to search for a broom and perhaps some aspirin. The blue flicker teased him again. He glanced over his shoulder and gasped. A bearded face radiated in the fire.

"Give up," it commanded. "No more pussy-footing. Join usssss."

Words clogged his throat, threatening to kill him. He swallowed, hoping to dislodge them. The broken glass captured his attention, and he silently swore not to drink again, no matter the number of women in the house.

"It is not a drinking problem," the voice echoed. "You are not human. Your troubles have lead you back to your ancestral home, to your place as Wisdom Keeper. Your life is meaningless here."

Alfred blinked. How easy it would be to blame fate for his problems. He'd not had children because he wasn't human. He'd not found a job because he already had one among a different race. Ha! But he knew better. His brother reminded him as often as a letter could reach him.

"I --- I've really lost it. Surely, I will wake up soon."

"Thissss is not a dream."

Alfred rubbed his eyes, the blue glare becoming intense.

"Face it, Sarah will not miss you. Your so-called brother will not miss you. Come closer, look and see," the voice demanded.

Then the flame dissolved like water dripping onto hot ashes and the bricks twisted in a spine-curdling pattern. The gaping mouth that remained held only darkness. Perhaps this was his way to freedom. The familiar darkness urged him forward, his feet crunching on the broken glass.

****

Who was Albert speaking too? Sarah tried hard to ignore the piercing eyes of the women around her, but they cut like knives. She went to pick up her tea cup again, but stopped mid reach at the crunch of glass coming from behind her. She rushed to the door and flung it open.

"Albert stop!" she cried, placing herself squarely in front of him. "Stop right now. Look, you're bleeding." She pointed to his stockinged feet, streaked red. Albert muttered her name and shook his head as though he'd come out of a trance. As he did, he bumped her. To gain her balance, Sarah wrapped her hands around her stomach and stepped back toward the fireplace.

Albert's eyes flew to her round middle, eyes clearing and jaw going slack. Sarah grinned. He'd returned to her. "You had me worried," she stated stepping carefully around the glass to press a kiss to his cheek. He held her a moment longer than normal. The slash of tree branches on the window made Sarah jump, and then she chuckled at herself.

****

Albert would never let her go. The strange circumstances that had lead him to consider death as an alternative vanished as he saw Sarah protect her midsection like an egg. He allowed her to pull away from him, and realized how this must look to her and the nosy faces peeking in behind her.

"I'm so sorry. I've made a mess of things again, haven't I?" he whispered, the echo of failure beating his skull with the remnants of his earlier headache.

"No, I'm just glad you're alright. Don't you dare do that again." Her voice soothed him, and she once again placed a hand on her middle just for a second. Was it his cruel imagination again? He mimicked her movement with his own fingers, and she rewarded him with a smile that sparkled from her soul.

"It's true," he stated. "You're with child?"

She nodded, her curls dancing about her face. "I didn't want to tell you until I'd made it further along to make sure this one would survive." A shadow cast over her features. He tucked her back into himself, wrapping his harms like a cocoon around her.

"What wonderful news," he murmured. "News worth living for."

Epilogue

From the Eyes of a Chief Justice

Excerpts from a letter written in 1948 By Marvin Rosenberry, Chief Justice of Wisconsin, Supreme Court. He was in Coeur d'Alene to attend the wedding of his niece Mary Jean Rosenbuerry and Joel Ferris.

Mr. Jewett had placed his house in Coeur d'Alene at the disposal of Walter and Sarah Maude. It is a large, roomy and most comfortable place. He maintains maids in the house and, in addition, Walter and Sarah Maude and their two girls and Walter III have spent almost the entire summer at their farm north of Little Falls...

Sunday Mr. Jewett came about 11:00 A.M. with his motor boat, which easily accommodates fifteen or twenty people, and took us for a ride up Coeur d'Alene Lake. We went up the lake several miles and anchored in a very beautiful bay. The young people who brought their swimming suits proceeded to take advantage of the opportunity. After swimming around for half an hour or so a very ice luncheon was served, which everybody enjoyed. Coeur d'Alene lake has very precipitous banks. We were anchored within about twenty-five feet of the shore, and the anchor line, which was fifty feet long just touched bottom. We spent a couple of hours there and then raised anchor and went to the Elder home on the lake about half way between the place where we anchored and the dock in front of the Jewett place, where we spent a short time visiting with the Elders. Mr. Elder is the leading lawyer of Coeur d'Alene, and when I was there in 1928 and '29, I became well acquainted with him. We then returned to the Jewett home and after changing our clothes, went to Mrs. John Gray's for a very lovely supper and a most pleasant evening...

Author Bios

Lila Bolme is on the state Board of Directors for Idaho Writer's League and serves as Vice President for the Coeur d'Alene chapter. She has won several awards for her short fiction and poetry, and is the current editor of the Lakegazette, the monthly newsletter of the Coeur d'Alene chapter.

"I'm the mother of 3 grown children who, for some reason, actually like me. Probably because I let them eat cookie dough when they were growing up. Thirty four years ago I was tricked into marriage by a guy with beer goggles and a six-pack, both of which eventually disappeared but he's still hangin' around because after all these years, he's convinced I'm on the verge of being able to cook something beside hashblacks and squasage. I write because I'm a wordy girl and because I want an excuse to leave the housework undone."

"A new writer, Becca Crouse enjoys creating short stories of any genre and is attempting to finish her first full length novel while drinking her weight in coffee."

Anna Goodwin is a former psychotherapist, lecturer and workshop presenter and has taught at two universities. In the recent years she has become a writer of both non-fiction and fiction books. She is the co-author of a renowned textbook on Sand Play Therapy later translated into Chinese, as well as the author of two self help books about Post Traumatic Stress. At present she is writing psychological suspense using her extensive knowledge of psychology and PTSD. She is also writing her father's story about his and his families escape from Russia to Canada during the revolution and the early Stalin purges.

For more information go to her website: www.anaparkergoodwin.com

Australian born Josephie Dean Jackson has been a resident of CdA for two years after she and her husband discovered this lakeside wonder three years ago. Starting out as a mental health professional, Dean Jackson was on a path to business law, however as life often goes, this path was sidetracked, for her it was by a move to the USA where ultimately a new career in O&G was formed, rounding out as COO of a highly successful Land & Mineral consulting practice she cofounded. A serial creator, Dean Jackson is also the first woman Tea Farmer in the USA, having founded the first Texas tea farm (2009) and is establishing one here in CdA; the designer of three apps and has many writings going at once, including a self-directed guideline for a new therapy modality she created incorporating Gongfucha and Sand Tray Therapy (Oct 2017) and part one of a stand-alone tea journal  (Aug 2017); "Mooz," a moose character whose stories teach children and parents, together, about the history and cultures of this region along with the beauty and value of asking questions, self-responsibility and insight (first 3 of the series, Sept 2017), and "The Diplomacy of Tea – A history of the economics and politics of the Queen of Herbs" is due mid 2019. Anything related all fields of science, foreign relations and cultural intelligence have always been passions of Dean Jackson. She is also the justifiably awed and proud mother of the most perfect, intelligent, accomplished and beautiful daughter in the world…ever…

Tana Lovett spent a nomadic childhood, routinely relocating all over Southern California, with her mother and two brothers. When she was eleven, they spent the school year in a rural Colorado town, homesteaded largely by Italian immigrants. This was potent fuel for her vivid, pre-teen imagination, and the memory grew over time into her first novel. Tana and her husband, Captain Awesome Man, live with a colony of Sugar Gliders in northern Idaho, surrounded by their big-fat-Mormon family.

She is President of IECRWA, and her debut novel For the Love of Chocolate is coming soon from Cedar Fort Publishing.

Cocolalla author Jennifer Lamont Leo writes historical fiction set in the early 20th century. Her first novel, You're the Cream in My Coffee, released in 2016, and an as-yet-untitled sequel is in the works. Visit her at www.jenniferlamontleo.com and on Facebook, Twitter, and Pinterest.

E.G. Moore is an award-winning poet and children's literature author, a freelance writer, and storyteller. She leads the local chapter of the Idaho Writers League and is the blog assistant for YAtopia. Her essay WEARING TERESA'S BOOTS is scheduled to be featured in Hope Paige's Anthology on loss in 2017. When she's not telling "Mommy Made stories" to her two daughters or working on her latest manuscript, she can be found either enjoying something from her to-read list with a glass of wine or in a plot-refreshing bubble bath. She's represented by Jessica Schmeidler of Golden Wheat Literary Agency.

www.emilygmoore.blogspot.com
www.facebook.com/EmilyGMooreWriter
www.twitter.com/EGMooreWriter

Terry Robinson is an award-winning author and published poet living in Coeur d'Alene. For over fifty years he has been spending his free time at Priest Lake Idaho, a lake on which he has found inspiration for a nearly complete book-length poetry manuscript capturing intimate private moments from his past. Terry shares some of his work on his blog: northidahostories.com.

Rostad, Barbara is a versatile writer with degrees in journalism and sociology. She has written for newspapers, taught English, speech and sociology at universities and schools in California, Idaho and Washington and currently writes for the Norwegian American. A member of IWL since 2000, she has won statewide contest awards, published articles and poems, edited both technical and literary works and compiled a book on cross-country skiing for the visually and mobility impaired.

Larry Telles, California born, and a resident of Dalton Gardens, Idaho for 18 years. Had a 30 year career with Pacific Bell as technical instructor and curriculum developer. Graduate of the Art Instruction School of Minneapolis, and former member of SCBWI. Graduated 1998 from Holy Names College, in Oakland, California, with BA degree in English, cum laude. Larry has written children's stories, and non-fiction and has three books published. Two on Silent film and one on Amateur Radio. In addition Larry has produced three DVDs. He spends some of his time as CEO of Bitterroot Mountain Publishing, where he does the formatting for both print and Kindle books, and creates covers. He is currently working on a series of documentaries for television on the silent serial queens who never received the recognition for their contribution to motion pictures.

Brother Music, AKA Jesse Warburton, has been playing music for over fifty years, both in the Untied States and around the world. This has given Brother Music a lot of experiences upon which to write. He particularly enjoys writing poetry and short stories about his own life. Jesse has recently created a new, fictional character – Blackjack Diamond, inspired by the life of boxing legend Jack Dempsey. One of only a few musicians who plays the **harp-guitar**, he is also one of the last of the traditional one-man bands in America. It's taken years for him to find the time to write. Now is the time.

THANK YOU FOR YOUR SUPPORT!

www.ingramcontent.com/pod-product-compliance
Lightning Source LLC
Chambersburg PA
CBHW060400050426
42449CB00009B/1827